Midnight Songs of Nasir Kazmi

100 Ghazals in English

Selected and Translated by
Gurupdesh Singh

BLUEROSE PUBLISHERS
India | U.K.

Copyright © Gurupdesh Singh 2024

All rights reserved by author. No part of this publication may be reproduced, stored in a retrieval system or transmitted in any form or by any means, electronic, mechanical, photocopying, recording or otherwise, without the prior permission of the author. Although every precaution has been taken to verify the accuracy of the information contained herein, the publisher assumes no responsibility for any errors or omissions. No liability is assumed for damages that may result from the use of information contained within.

BlueRose Publishers takes no responsibility for any damages, losses, or liabilities that may arise from the use or misuse of the information, products, or services provided in this publication.

For permissions requests or inquiries regarding this publication, please contact:

BLUEROSE PUBLISHERS
www.BlueRoseONE.com
info@bluerosepublishers.com
+91 8882 898 898
+4407342408967

ISBN: 978-93-5989-332-7

Cover design: Muskan Sachdeva
Cover photo of Nasir Kazmi by Basir Kazmi

First Edition: January 2024

Message

It has always been my strong wish to see the works of my father, Nasir Kazmi, translated into other languages. Twenty years ago fellow poet Dr Debjani Chatterjee and I jointly translated twenty-five of Nasir's ghazals into English. These translations were published in various magazines and anthologies. Now it's gratifying to see that Gurupdesh Singh has translated a hundred of Nasir's ghazals into English. I really appreciate the enthusiasm, the selection, and the hard work that he has put in to achieve his goal. I'm confident that his work will be received with interest and will be widely acknowledged. I wish him all the best.

Basir Sultan Kazmi
Son of Basir Kazmi

CONTENTS

	page
Translator's Note	11
Introduction	17

Ghazals

1. aaj to be-sabab udaas hai jee	52
1. Heart feels sad today for no good reason	53
2. aaj tujhe kyun chup si lagi hai	54
2. Why are you sunk in silence so deep	55
3. ab un se aur taqaza-e-baada kya karta	56
3. More of this wine I wouldn't ask for me	57
4. ai hamsukhan wafa ka taqaaza hai ab yahi	58
4. Friends, loyalty now has for us new scripts	59
5. apni dhun men rahta hun	62
5. I stay lost in myself	63
6. araaish-e-khayal bhi ho dil-kusha bhi ho	64
6. A thought ought to be beautiful and moving too	65
7. avvalin chand ne kya baat sujhaayi mujh ko	68
7. The sight of the new moon is a dead ringer	69
8. bane banaye hue raaston pe ja nikle	70
8. They took the path that was much travelled	71
9. basa huya hai khayalon men koyi paikar-e-naaz	72
9. Someone of a gentle bearing occupies my mind	73
10. beganavaar unse mulaqaat ho to ho	76
10. Like strangers, I may meet her, if at all	77
11. chand gharaanon ne mil-jul kar	78
11. A few families with their joint might	79
12. dafatan dil men kisi yaad ne li angdaayi	80
12. In my heart a memory suddenly took a turn	81
13. dayar-e-dil ki raat men charagh sa jala gaya	82
13. Someone lit a candle in the dark corner of my heart	83

14.	dekh mohabbat ka dastoor	84
	14. Look at love and its way	85
15.	dil dhadakne ka sabab yaad aaya	86
	15. Why the heart missed a beat, I know	87
16.	dil men aur to kya rakha hai	88
	16. In heart, what else can be new	89
17.	dil men ik lehar si uthi hai abhi	90
	17. Something like a tide surged in me now	91
18.	dukh ki lehar ne chheda hoga	94
	18. A swirl of pain may have started it	95
19.	fikr-e-taamir-e-aashiyan bhi hai	98
	19. If I have worries about making a nest	99
20.	gaa raha tha koyi darakhaton men	100
	20. I heard someone croon in the trees	101
21.	gali gali abaad thi jin se kahan gaye vo log	104
	21. Who kept the streets abuzz, where are they	105
22.	gali gali meri yaad bichhi hai	106
	22. Step cautiously, remains of me are spread all the way	107
23.	gaye dinon ka suragh le kar	108
	23. With intimations of the past he came	109
24.	gham hai ya khushi hai tu	112
	24. Grief or joy, what are you	113
25.	girafta-dil hain bahut aaj tere deewane	114
	25. Your crazy lovers are now captives of their heart	115
26.	ham jis ped kee chhaanv men baitha karate the	116
	26. The shade tree we use to sit under	117
27.	haasil-e-ishq tera husn-e-pasheman hi sahi	118
	27. Let your mortified beauty be the gain of love	119
28.	hoti hai tere naam se vahshat kabhi kabhi	120
	28. Your name brings revulsion at times	121
29.	husn ko dil men chhupa kar dekho	122
	29. Keep secrets of beauty in your heart	123
30.	in sahme hue shahron ki faza kuchh kahti hai	124
	30. The petrified state of these cities says something	125
31.	ishq jab zamzama-paira hoga	126
	31. When love sings in all its resplendence	127
32.	ishq men jeet huyi ya maat	130
	32. In love, did you lose or gain?	131

33.	is se pahle ki bichhad jaayen ham	132
	33. Before we decide to split forever	133
34.	jabin pe dhoop si ankhon men	134
	34. Those sunny eyes on your face have some coyness	135
35.	jab zara tez hava hoti hai	136
	35. When there is that fierce wind	137
36.	Jalwa-saaman hai rang-o-boo ham se	140
	36. Colour and smell owe their glory to us	141
37.	jo guftni nahin vo baat bhi sunaa dunga	142
	37. I'll speak what I am not supposed to speak	143
38.	jurm-e-inkar ki sazaa hi de	144
	38. For saying no, order a punishment for me	145
39.	kab talak muddaa kahe koyi	146
	39. How long can one insist on his say	147
40.	kal jinhen zindagi thi raas bahut	148
	40. Yesterday, those who rejoiced in life	149
41.	kaarvan sust rahbar khamosh	150
	41. Caravan sluggish, the guide in silence	151
42.	kaun us raah se guzarta hai	152
	42. Who, I guess, will pass by this lane	153
43.	khayal-e-tark-e-tamanna na kar sake tu bhi	156
	43. Hope you too won't give up on your passion	157
44.	kise dekhen kahan dekha na jaaye	158
	44. Where can I look for who I can't see	159
45.	kisi ka dard ho dil beqaraar apna hai	160
	45. Whoever is in pain, my heart goes into unrest	161
46.	kisi kali ne bhi dekha na aankh bhar ke mujhe	162
	46. No look of longing from a new blossom for me	163
47.	kuchh to ehsas-e-ziyan tha pahle	164
	47. Earlier too, a slight feel of waste I had	165
48.	kuchh yadgar-e-shahr-e-sitamgar hi le chalen	168
	48. Let us carry a souvenir from the city of the callous	169
49.	kya zamana tha ki ham roz mila karte the	170
	49. What good days were those when we met daily	171
50.	kyun gham-e-raftagan kare koyi	172
	50. Why would one cry for those departed	173
51.	mahroom-e-khwab dida-e-hairan na tha kabhi	174
	51. My curious eyes were never so bereft of dreams	175

52.	main hun raat ka ek baja hai	176
	52. It is me in the night one o'clock	177
53.	main is shahar men kyon aaya tha	180
	53. Why did I turn to this city	181
54.	main ne jab likhna sikha tha	182
	54. When I learnt the writing code	183
55.	mujh ko aur kahin jaana tha	184
	55. I had to go another direction	185
56.	mumkin nahin mata-e-sukhan mujh se chheen le	188
	56. No way can he take away my power to articulate	189
57.	musalsal bekali dil ko rahi hai	190
	57. Heart had its restlessness all the time	191
58.	naye kapde badal kar jaun kahan	192
	58. Who should I get dressed up for and have my hair blown	193
59.	nasib-e-ishq dil-e-beqaraar bhi to nahin	194
	59. Neither the bliss of love, nor a restless heart	195
60.	'nasir' kya kahta phirta hai kuchh na suno to behtar hai	198
	60. Whatever 'Nasir' says, if you listen not, it is better	199
61.	naaz-e-begaanagi men kya kuchh tha	200
	61. Her conceited unconcern had a lot in it	201
62.	niyyat-e-shauq bhar na jaye kahin	202
	62. What if love gets full and fades away	203
63.	o mere masroof khuda	204
	63. Oh, my busy busy Lord!	205
64.	parde men har awaaz ke shamil to vahi hai	206
	64. The one hidden in every voice is the same	207
65.	patthar ka vo shahr bhi kya tha	208
	65. All of stone it was, what a city	209
66.	phool khushboo se juda hai ab ke	210
	66. Fragrance leaves the flowers this time	211
67.	qahr se dekh na har aan mujhe	212
	67. Don't you with stern eyes look at me	213
68.	rah-e-junoon men khirad ka hawaala kya karta	214
	68. Why talk of reason in the state of obsession	215
69.	rah-navard-e-bayabaan-e-gham sabr kar sabr kar	216
	69. Swirling in the wilderness of woes, keep patience	217
70.	rang barsaat ne bhare kuchh to	220
	70. The rain brought a cheer a little bit	221

71.	rang dikhlati hai kyaa-kyaa umr ki raftaar bhi	222
	71. How many shades ageing shows in colour	223
72.	raunaqen theen jahan men kya kya kuchh	224
	72. What joyous times the world had, imagine	225
73.	safar-e-manzil-e-shab yaad nahin	226
	73. The Night march to our post, I remember not	227
74.	sar men jab ishq ka sauda na raha	230
	74. When the madness of love in me left	231
75.	saz-e-hasti ki sadaa ghaur se sun	232
	75. The ringing call of life, listen with care	233
76.	shahr-dar-shahr ghar jalaaye gaye	236
	76. Cities after cities, homes were set on fire	237
77.	shahr sunsaan hai kidhar jaayen	238
	77. The town is desolate, where can I go	239
78.	shuaan-e-husn tere husn ko chhupaati thi	240
	78. Glowing rays of beauty veiled your visage	241
79.	so gayi shahr ki har ek gali	242
	79. The city is asleep so is its every street	243
80.	sunaata hai koyi bhooli kahaani	246
	80. Someone tells a tale long lost	247
81.	tanhai ka dukh gahra tha	251
	81. The pain of loneliness was deep set	252
82.	tere aane ka dhoka sa raha hai	254
	82. I had a faint idea of your coming	255
83.	tere khayaal se lo de uthi hai tanhai	256
	83. A flashback of you has lit up my solitary existence	257
84.	tere milne ko bekal ho gaye hain	260
	84. To meet you they seem to be excited	261
85.	teri nigah ke jaadu bikharte jaate hain	262
	85. The magic of your eyes has started fading	263
86.	teri zulfon ke bikharne ka sabab hai koyi	264
	86. Not for nothing you have ruffled hair	265
87.	tu asir-e-bazm hai ham-sukhan	266
	87. O friend, you are a captive of your camp	267
88.	tujh bin ghar kitna soona tha	268
	88. How bleak was home without you	269
89.	tum aa gaye ho to kyun intizaar-e-shaam Karen	270
	89. Since you are here, why wait for the evening	271

90.	vo dil-nawaaz hai lekin nazar-shanaas nahin	272
	90. He can console but not read eyes and tell	273
91.	vo is ada se jo aaye to kyun bhala na lage	274
	91. Why wouldn't it feel good the way she came	275
92.	vo sahilon pe gaane vaale kya huye	278
	92. Those who sang on the banks, where are they	279
93.	yaad aata hai roz-o-shab koyi	280
	93. I long to see someone night and day	281
94.	ye bhi kya shaam-e-mulaqaat aayi	282
	94. What an evening it was to meet	283
95.	ye raat tumhari hai chamakte raho taaro	284
	95. O stars! The night is all yours, keep shining	285
96.	ye shab ye khayal-o-khwab tere	286
	96. Images, dreams of you at night	287
97.	ye sitam aur ki ham phool kahen kharon ko	288
	97. Cruel it is, if we are asked to call spikes flowers	289
98.	yun tere husn ki tasveer ghazal men aaye	290
	98. Portrait of your beauty enters into my verse	291
99.	zaban sukhan ko sukhan bankpan ko tarsega	292
	99. Speech will long for words and words for delicacy	293
100.	Assorted verses from Pehli Baarish	294
	100. Assorted verses from Pehli Baarish	295

Translator's Note

Translator's job is akin to that of a computer programmer. He may have the program running, but no amount of meticulous or comprehensive input can make it impervious to subsequent revisions or updates. The task becomes rather thankless or even worthless when it comes to poetry; more so, when the two involved languages have such a wide gap as east and west. We have seen the confusion or the disaster that such an attempt can cause with respect to such a classical poet as Ghalib. It is not just the love for Ghalib's poetry that has afforded us sometimes as many as 20 translations of the same couplet. At the bottom of this all is a sense of dissatisfaction with earlier versions or a sort of competitive drive to show 'It can be done better' or a bit of charitable energy to give the poem or poet a better justice. But unfortunately none of the competitors ever succeed in making it up to the magic of the original.

With such a trepidation in mind I started this work and with an equal or more apprehension I present it now to the readers for their appraisal. My only consolation is that unlike Ghalib I do not have many competitors. Earlier in 2003 an attempt was made in England to present 25 of his ghazals in free verse for the English readers without reference to the originals (Generations of Ghazal edited and translated by Debjani Chatterjee and Basir Kazmi). This is the first time that such a major chunk of his work would be translated in English for readers of languages other than Urdu. In any case, it is better to have a contested translation than no translation at all. The task of reaching out to the alien readers that a translated work does is, without doubt, of immense significance and a global necessity in the present times of melting cultures and intercontinental communication. Nasir Kazmi has won hearts of Urdu and Hindi lovers with his sensitive portrayal of human emotions and conditions both in cordial and conflicting times. He, by all means, deserves a much extended audience, especially of the Indian subcontinent where despite cultural affinities, linguistic diversity abounds in plenty.

Translation is never an easy task we know that, but translating Urdu poetry in English has some peculiar difficulties that I, like other translators, faced. On top of it, for no bigger reason than to keep the poetic feel intact, I decide to do the conversion in rhyme. It has added a few extra miles to my journey to the other end. In all, I have tried only two rhyme schemes - the standard ghazal format AA, BA, CA and the heroic couplet AA, BB, CC. The choice was largely dependent on the possible thematic unity of the ghazal couplets. If they showed some kind of strong rhyming unity or continuity of a theme, then the choice was the conventional ghazal rhyme, otherwise they were given the form of stand-alone couplets.

Poetry translators usually confront two sets of problems – one linguistic and the other thematic. Poetry being translucent about its meaning usually demands its readers to make a bit of guesswork about the language used to arrive at a plausible meaning. In a way, the problem is largely linguistic as interpretation is the outcome of readers' struggle with the poetic language.

The dominant trope of all good poetry is its ambiguity of reference. The poetic language being rhetorical and laconic rarely makes it clear what context the poem belongs to. The poem brings up this obscurity with the help of a language that has no clear referents. Poets of repute are past masters at deliberately deploying a language that adds layers of meaning to their verses. The language of romance, for example, has been used by different poets in Urdu to refer, besides love, to spiritual existence or political ideology or general humanistic concerns. Every lexical item, therefore, in the syntax including common structural terms like interrogatives, negatives, connectives, deictics etc. carries the inherent load of multiple interpretations.

We can easily see how pronouns and other deictic terms, like here, there, today or tomorrow that demand a situational referents to make meaning, are the usual culprits. (More will be said about them in the Introduction). Translating them in another language seems no problem, but in Urdu they generate a lot of confusion; pronouns in particular, in terms of corresponding gender and number equivalents, even when this language, unlike English, indicates them in multiple inflections to other parts of the speech. One obvious example of this confusion is the second or third person pronoun used for the beloved or friend. There is no he or she in Urdu, only a common pronoun *'vo'* for third person and *'tu'* for second person which stand for both genders and both numbers (the plural form is used also for the honorific singular). In Urdu ghazal particularly, it has been a long standing practice to use the masculine inflections in the entire syntax even when referring to a female beloved. Thus, the translator is left to make decisions about such matters, keeping in mind the level of intimacy that the couplet or ghazal displays. You may, therefore, find shifting gender pronouns for the same term in different ghazals in this collection. Similarly, Urdu has a first person pronoun *'ham'* which can stand for both singular and plural first person. Again the English translation here may have 'I' or 'we' depending upon the way a verse has been interpreted. The problem becomes more acute with the second person, especially in the signature verses where its use in the original may not always refer to the other person but to the speaker himself, as the speech situation may be monologic in tone.

The other grammatical issue that teases a translator of Indian languages is the subjectless construction. It is much easier to omit the subject or front the predicate in a sentence in our languages than it is in English. For example, it is perfectly fine to say 'kahaan ja rahe ho?' in Hindi or Urdu, but it would be odd to translate it as 'where going?' in English. We have to insert the subject 'you' to make it sound normal. In poetry, such subjectless sentences create a linguistic ambiguity which the translator has to sometimes make up by supplying the implied subject. Take, for example, the following couplet which has no subject in the original but has been provided one in the translated version

bhari duniya men ji nahin lagta
jaane kis cheez ki kami hai abhi (17)
I don't feel at home in this teeming world
I don't know what I want, what I miss now
Nasir Kazmi's poetry offers many such instances where the reader has to imagine or provide a subject or an object to make sense of the syntax.

Similies, metaphors and metonymic terms are the standard stuff of any poetry, but unfortunately they are highly contiguous to the linguistic culture they belong to. Outside their culture they may sound meaningless or connote meanings that are alien to them. Much of this metaphorical lexicon is a part of the popular language used by natives in their everyday conversation. The poet exploits this familiarity with language in a subtle way to extend the bounds of meanings by placing them in contexts which are new or unexpected. Thus, such common poetical tropes as *chaman* (garden) or *kafila* (a group of travellers) or *manzil* (destination) assume meanings which no longer remain familiar. In fact, their repeated use in different contexts makes it doubly difficult for the translator to find exact equivalents for them.

The moral dilemma with the translator is whether to kill the metaphor and focus on the meaning or to retain the metaphor and make the verse inaccessible to non-native readers. Urdu poetry is replete with such common, yet chameleon metaphors which change their meanings with every new use. Therefore, you may find words like *wafaa* (loyality), *bekhudi* (not being oneself), *qaid* (imprisonment), *razdaan* (secret sharer), *aanchal* (a scarf or shawl), just to mention a few, translated differently in different contexts. One can imagine, if a native reader will have to make a special effort to contextualize a particular lexical item, then how problematic it would be to transfer that in another language. In many cases, I have, however, retained and translated the metaphorical image literally believing that it would be accessible to the alient reade as it is. Or, it would be equally relishing for readers of other languages to get familiar with a native literary tropes and its syntactic construction.

The language of poetry is economical and at times cryptic too, especially when grammatical linkers are omitted or a parallel of ideas is drawn. The underlying network of semantic relations which is obvious to the native readers may not seem so easy to the readers of another language. In the English version of many a passages here, therefore, readers may find that connectives and other pointers have been added to make the syntax more coherent in showing the implied meanings. Such liberties are the compulsions of translation. On the other hand, traditional Urdu poetry consciously avoids punctuation marks to build a rhetorical thrust at the time of recitation or to facilitate ambiguity of intent. This happens particularly in interrogative constructions which may not always stand for questions. If the reader finds too many interrogation signs missing in the translated text, they must pardon me as it has been deliberately done to respect the original syntax.

In spite of these usual hurdles, I must say it was a pleasure translating Nasir. His poetry I hope will give solace to many a bruised hearts, restore faith in the romance of life and provide sustenance in the face of despair and crisis.

To conclude, I would like to thank all those who have been helpful in bringing this effort to fruition. First among them, of course, is Basir Kazmi who holds the copyrights of his father Nasir Kazmi's writings and permitted me to use them. Not only this, he offered to go through some selected texts, made suggestions and encouraged me to extend the anthology to 100 ghazals. (Earlier, I don't know for what mystical reasons I had decided to stop at 85.) Being an eminent and a well-decorated poet himself, Basir Kazmi is meticulous in his poetic craft and as compiler and editor of his father's works, he understands his poetry from a much closer angle than anyone else. I have no bigger words of gratitude for him except 'a big thank you' for his enormous help and the kind words that he has sent as acknowledgment to this anthology.

Rekhta.org is the major source where I was able to get most of Nasir's ghazals. Diamond books publication *Main Kahan Chala Gaya* also provided a number of ghazals included in this anthology. I am grateful to these organisations for their primary help.

I am also obliged to many of my friends, Dr.Rajesh Sharma, Dr.Swaraj Raj, Dr.Harbir Singh, Dr.Rahul Sharma, Dr.Gurpartap Khairah, Prof. Sunita Dhillon, Prof. Mohan Singh, Prof. Manbir Bhullar, Dr. Aziz Abbas for their help in interpreting and revising some of the earlier versions.

And finally to my wife, who provided me all the help in those long spells of seclusion when I was cooped up in my study working to make this book a reality.

Gurupdesh Singh

INTRODUCTION

Syed Raza Nasir Kazmi

Nasir Kazmi died young, but his poems did not. In fact, they are growing in stature every passing day. He was published more after his death than during his lifetime. Majority of his poems were anthologised after he died in 1972 and ever since have become the voice of millions of sensitive souls who find this world too much or too little to their liking. You can call him a downright romantic, a melancholic, a brooding loner or a child who loses his sand castle in the evening tide and hopes to find it with the rise of the Sun. To me, he is a bridge that connects us to our past, a portrait that mirrors our age-lines, a voice that we hear after the thunder of the day is done. His imagery speaks of loss, alienation, nostalgia, grief, fleeting love and inhospitable environs, particularly those obtained after the Partition. A contemporary of such Pakistani stalwarts as Faiz Ahmed Faiz, Munir Niazi, Ahmed Nadeem Kasmi, he succeeded in making a distinct place for himself due to his simple diction and lilting lyricism.

Life

Born in 1925 at Ambala (India), he continued his education both this side and across the border before it was created; his father being in the British Indian army. He finished his matriculation from a school in Ambala and then moved to Lahore for his college education, came back in 1945 and continued living in Ambala until 1947 when his family decided to migrate to Pakistan, where they soon settled in Lahore. Until his death in 1972, Lahore remained his favourite haunt as it was there that he started his career, spent his working years, enjoyed the company of other men of letters, made night sorties in its streets and strolled in its green riverside surroundings.

Though Nasir Kazmi remained gainfully employed in Lahore from 1952 until his end, yet the real occupation for him was writing. His poetry and his life are so intensely enmeshed that it is difficult to tell them apart. He loved everything that art is all about – music, literature, nature; that is why probably he entered into professions which are akin to literary pursuits. As a young man he also tried to learn to play sitar and sarangi, but couldn't pursue it in later years. In 1952, he started his career in journalism as staff editor and slowly rose to become chief editor of a couple of popular journals of his time. From 1959 to 1964, he was editor of the state journal *Hum Log*. In between he also worked as Liaison Officer in the department of social security and assistant publicity officer in another. Then, in 1964, with the help of his mentor and a senior friend, Hafiz Hoshiarpuri, he joined Radio Pakistan and continued there till his death in 1972.

He died young, but the volume of his work belies this. Unfortunately most of his works were published after his demise. During his life time he was able to publish one anthology of poems called *Burg e Nai* and that too at the young age of 27. In fact, he started writing in 1940 and by the time he reached college in Lahore he was already a popular poet as was confirmed in the annual *mushairas* that he participated. In those days he used to sing his poetry or recite it in rhythm. His poetry was romantic in nature and, some believe, was written in imitation of the more popular Akhtar Shirani, though on his own admission he was more influenced by the poetry of Mir Taqi Mir and Hafiz Hoshiarpuri. It is often said that he learnt poetry from Hafiz Hoshiarpuri, who was himself a recognised poet and also the Director General of Radio Pakistan at that time. But after his death, when his diary journals were published it came to light that he considered his mother a real teacher, and then also admits that he consulted Hafiz from time to time.

Burg e Nai was the real success that made Nasir Kazmi popular with the masses. Even today any anthology that represents his work cannot be considered complete without including many of its ghazals. In the present anthology too, a substantial number of ghazals have been taken from *Burg e Nai*. It is difficult to say who established Nasir Kazmi as a niche poet: the critics or the musicians. It is no mere coincidence that Nasir is one of the most sung of Pakistani Urdu poets. He is the darling of almost every celebrated ghazal singer. And interestingly, most of the ghazals that have been picked up for musical rendition come from *Burg e Nai*. His poetry instantly strikes a responsive chord with a delicate mind.

dil dhadakne ka sabab yaad aaya
vo teri yaad thi ab yaad aaya (15)
Why the heart missed a beat, I know
A thought of you gave a knock, I know
(*Ghulam Ali-Asha Bhonsle*)

kisi kali ne bhi dekha na aankh bhar ke mujhe
guzar gai jaras-e-gul udaas kar ke mujhe (46)
No look of longing from a new blossom for me
Convoys of spring came but only saddened me
(*Abida Parveen*)

Though ghazal remained the preferred genre with Nasir Kazmi, he also tried his hand at nazm under the influence of Progressive movement and published in 1957 his major nazm 'Nishat e Khwab'. His other writings published after his death include his Diwan (1972) and *Pehli Baarish* (1975) a rare and masterly experiment in short meter (*chhotee behar*) where he has written a collection of 25 ghazals in that form on a single rhyme. It is a highly evocative package of poems that portrays the landscape of his memories which actually constitutes his poetic imagination. *Nishat-e-Khawab* (1977) is a full collection of his nazms. *Sur ki Chhaya* (1981) is a poetic drama *Khushk Chashme ke Kinaare* (1982) is a collection of his prose writings, essays, radio features, interviews, editorials etc. *Chand Preshan Kagaz* (1995) comprises the leftover parts of his diary, as he had lost some volumes during transition from India to Pakistan. In admiration of and as tribute to his favourite poets he had also made a special selection of their poetry which got published as Intekhab-e-Meer (1989); Intekhab-e-Nazeer (1990); Intekhab-e-Wali Dakni (1991); Intekhab-e-Insha (1991). Most of these posthumous publications were the love's labour of his two sons Basir Sultan Kazmi and Hassan Sultan Kazmi. Basir is an academic and has taught in a number of Universities in UK and is himself a well recognised, award winning poet.

References to Nasir Kazmi in books, articles and interviews have created a folklore about his long chatting sessions at coffee or tea houses, his love for common people, his conversational skills, his chain smoking, pan chewing, his late night walks back home. All of these must be true, as the two portraits, one fictional and one real, that I will like to present here confirm these aspects of his personality. The fictional account comes from an eminent partition play of the 1980's.

Prof. Syed Asghar Wajahat's famous play *Jis Lahore Nai Dekhya O Jamiya Hi Nahi (*One is not born yet if he hasn't been to Lahore*)* has a character by the name Nasir Kazmi, who, notwithstanding the fictional nature of the drama, is presented as the real life poet Nasir Kazmi. The author also authenticates it by making the character a poet in the play and getting him to recite a number of his real poems. The story revolves around fundamentalist and moderate Muslims when they have to deal with the eviction of an old Hindu lady from her house and ultimately her death in the aftermath of partition. Nasir Kazmi figures prominently in this play — in seven scenes out of eighteen. Barring one or two scenes, Nasir, the character has been shown either sitting or hanging around a tea shop. On a couple of occasions, it is either midnight or the early morning which, in fact, is the other end of the night for Nasir. When it comes to reading his poems, his best audience is the tea shop owner or his tonga (horse car) driver. In between his dialogues he also throws a couplet from Mir. His wit and sarcasm comes best when he is confronted with a fundamentalist bully who neither knows religion nor empathy. Being en émigré himself, Nasir understands the religious differences between Hindus and Muslims, yet the feelings of cultural affinity that he experienced before partition make him compassionate and he shows them when the last rites of the old Hindu lady are performed.

The play deals amply with the poet character Nasir, who again matches very closely to the real life poet Nasir Kazmi, about his views on poetry. Nasir in scene eight spends the whole night rambling on a tonga and writes a five stanza ghazal. When the tea vender asks why he does not sleep, Nasir tells that night is the prime time of creativity when flowers brew their juices, the sea turns its tides, fragrances are born and angels descend on the earth. Writing poetry, according to the poet character, is not a limited-hour job, it is a 24 hour occupation. In scene eleven, he tells that when he gets nostalgic, he can't stay indoors. And writing poetry is something that gives him the highest pleasure; he loves organising his inner world and translating his surroundings into words that can move hearts.

In scene thirteen, again he is on a walk alone, lost in his muse, when his friend meets him on the way. On asking why he was talking to fallen leaves, he tells that autumn is a season of gloom when trees shed their dry leaves; and he joins them in their time of misery. Nasir's friend, also a migrant, enquires him about a black bird that he had not seen in Lahore since he left India, Nasir, as usual, waxes poetic and says *"discovering that bird was more important to me than understanding progressive and Islamic literature. Initially when I came to Pakistan, I was interested in finding all those things that I loved from the core of my heart. I dearly loved mustard flowers and asked local people if they had those flowers in Lahore the same way as they have in India. I also enquired whether this place had spells of monsoon, the peacock dances and a colourful spring sky."* (*translated from the original*)

The preceding description is that of a character in the play, but in actual it matches wholly with the poet Nasir Kazmi whose life-long friend Intizar Hussain has provided us with many snippets of his life and interests. The Government of Pakistan issued a commemorative postage stamp in his honour in 2013. Reporting on one of these celebration events where he spoke, Hussain writes in his column in The Dawn of March 10, 2013 that rather than bulbul which is not a living bird, Kazmi would talk about the living birds like koel. Remember the black bird in the play and *fakhta* (dove). Hussain writes further

'Birds and trees don't come to him via a literary tradition but through his relationship with nature. This relationship was so powerful for him that on one occasion, feeling bored with his contemporaries

Kazmi declared, "the blooming mustard flower is my only contemporary."

Trees, birds, seasons, stars, the moon and the sun all come alive in his verses. Thanks to his imaginative eye, they all share friendly relationships with him. He is the most happy when in their company. Perhaps it is because his personality appears to be a continuation of his poetry. He writes poetry and at the same time lives poetry. He is a pedestrian wandering from street to street. It is at night, or to be more exact, in the hours after midnight that he feels free and hence happy wandering aimlessly, appearing to be in direct communion with the stars and the moon'.

In another article written earlier for a blogspot *'baithak'* on November 1, 2005, Intizar Hussain speaks about a meeting held in memory of Nasir Kazmi on his 32nd death anniversary. Many speakers recalled his night journeys and spoke about the time they spent with him patrolling the lanes of Lahore, sharing midnight tea sessions and watching him speak like an inspired creative person. Hussain sums up

'Nasir Kazmi was a perennial nocturnal wanderer. He wandered aimlessly but not thoughtlessly. He had devised a theory justifying his wanderings. The cosmos, he thought, had come into existence in the deep, dark hours of the night. Those hours are pregnant with the possibilities of a supreme creative act. I cannot, he said, afford to waste my time in sleep during these precious hours. And for years, he availed these precious hours to the full. It was only in the small hours when the birds began chirping that he felt sleepy and thought of returning home'.

He further clarifies that Nasir's relationship with night was not romantic but realistic. "*With the approach of night, the roads and streets grew quieter. And as the nocturnal hours passed by, quietness touched with a sense of peacefulness seemed to pervade the whole atmosphere inspiring the poet to say: Khali rasta bol raha hai"*

One of the most quoted references about Nasir Kazmi is the last television interview he gave to Intizar Hussain from his hospital bed. Here he speaks about his art, interests, hobbies.

'Horse riding, hunting, wandering in a village, walking along the river side, visiting mountains etc. were my favourite pastimes and probably this was the time when my mind got nourishment for loving nature and getting close to the expression of poetry. All my hobbies are related with fine arts, like singing, poetry, hunting, chess, love of birds, love of trees. ... I started writing poetry because I used to reflect that all the beautiful things, those I see and those in nature are not in my hands, and they go away from me. Few moments of time which die, cannot be made alive, I think can come alive in poetry that is why I (Nasir) started writing poetry!'
(https://www.wikiwand.com/en/Nasir_Kazmi; This part of the Interview is also available on the youtube)

In this interview Nasir speaks at length about his home, his progress as poet and his relationship with common people. He tells that in childhood atmosphere at home was conducive to studies. He had plenty of books at home including the Quran and those of Sheikh Sadi and Firdausi; he on his own had read Mir and Anees; his grandfather was fond of music. In his early teens he wrote his first couplet which he recalls was
Kabool hai jinhen gham bhi teri khushi ke liye
wo ji rahen hai haqeeqat mein zindagi ke liye
Those who love to accept pain for your sake
Are the ones who in reality live for life's sake
Nasir tells that he was so much pleased with it that if anything else had given him the same pleasure he would have never done poetry.

Talking to Intizar Hussain he recalls his very special relationship with a tongawala, who had died recently. The foundation of this friendship was laid on a particular rainy night when Nasir asked him to take him home and he refused as he had refused many others before him. But when Nasir told him that he was a poet and recited him a couplet, he was so pleased that he not only readily agreed to

carry him, but also promised to drive him the rest of his life and that too without charging. The couplet that Nasir recited was this
Waqya ye hai ke badnaam huye
Baat itni si hai ke aansoo nikla
The story is I earned notoriety
Merely because I shed a tear

Over the years many of those tonga-pullers became taxi drivers and Nasir continued to have the best of their love. He tells Intizar Hussain that on hearing the news of his ill health, a group of taxi drivers came to meet him in the hospital and even offered him monetary help which, of course, he refused.

As part of that interaction with Nasir Kazmi, Intizar Hussain also interviewed the owner of that old coffee house, which was a sort of cultural hub in those days. It had a great atmosphere for writers, thinkers, poets and journalists to have informal meetings and poetry sessions. The owner tells that Nasir's fame touched new heights after this couplet
ai dost ham ne tark-e-mohabbat ke bavajood
mahsoos ki hai teri zaroorat kabhi kabhi
O my dear! even after giving up on love
I have felt your absence and need at times (28.7)
According to him, Nasir was a hardworking poet. He had bits of pencils in his pocket and would write on scrap papers or the back of cigarette packets when inspired. He used to spend all day in the coffee house and continued smoking, chewing *paan* and having coffee incessantly.

Referring to the same interview on a special programme organised in the memory of Nasir Kazmi in 2013, Tashie Zaheer President, Urdu Academy of North America also recalls what Nasir Kazmi had to say about the creative act. According to him, poetry is not something written in meter. It is a way of looking at life, examining things from a certain point of view; and to express that in a harmonious way is poetry. Kazmi could see this attitude in the minor most workers such as a railway engine driver or a signal operator. Like a poet, he knows when to open or shut the gate. If he does not, it will result in a

disaster. A poet thinks of all humanity in general, believing if it was good for others then it must be good for him. Wherever people are creative in work, poetry happens. For this everyone has to take up the risk of solitary confinement. The fabric of poetry is woven with solitude and a tender heart. (translated from Tashie Zaheer's urdu speech)
(https://www.youtube.com/watch?v=ua_MhRdHmGE&feature=youtu.be)

Reading Poetry

The portraits above present him as a contemplative sensitive soul, a lover of nature and arts, and a night bird, yet at the same time he was a community man who loved the company of his friends, a commoner who could communicate and befriend anyone without any class considerations or intellectual pretensions. His poetry too had all of these traits where he expressed his innermost feelings and ideas without any intellectual or literary burden. Unlike the great poets of earlier times, he rarely tried to persianise his poetry. His language, his images and metaphors are simple direct and modern, though they do not always make it easy for the reader to catch the poetic import. His simplicity is deceptive and so is his lyricism which is so overwhelming that it sways the reader and makes him stay with its glossy surface without realising the riches that lie underneath.

Theoretically speaking, poetry of every kind runs into this risk, as it is not the lyricism or the romance of words that leads us away, it is the basic nature of the poetry indeed that it hides more than it reveals. The language of poetry, though seems like the ordinary, following the same syntactic rules, does not convey its meanings the same way as the day-to-day conversation or a journalistic write-up does. Poetic language weaves a pattern or configures a syntax that connotes much more by its tone, diction, rhyme and rhetoric than the sum total of its literal components. By the subtle use of any one or more of these elements, the poet impregnates his words with meanings that call out their significance, notwithstanding the direct reference those elements make. That is why Wainwright (in <u>Poetry The Basics</u>) calls all poetry 'gestural'. It leads you indirectly to its meanings. The corollary is that a poem makes gestures towards its meanings not the meaning. A poem is a multi-layered, polysemic entity.

One of the reasons, why poetry deals with indirections, can be found in the special use that poetry makes of certain language techniques. The way it builds parallels with the help of similes and metaphors or utilises words or images as symbols, poetry acquires a depth that makes readers go far beyond the literal and urge them to invest their literary or worldly knowledge to reach its hidden reserves of meaning. The poets have a special knack of turning the most ordinary of words or images into a complex network of implications. Nasir Kazmi also agrees
hujum-e-nasha-e-fikr-e-sukhan men
badal jaate hain lafzon ke maani
In the heady rush of poetic musings
Words undergo a change in meanings (80.7)

Wordsworth long ago spoke of them as the 'family language of poets'. In Urdu poetry some of the frequently recurring tropes like *manzil, ishq, safar, hizr, kinara* etc. are the stable members of this family language. The serious reader of Urdu poetry finds it highly useful to apply his historical knowledge of the use of these stock images to confirm or deny a particular meaning or to contextualise a poetic event or to recognise the emotional and ideational load of a verse. Eliot calls this faculty of the reader his awareness of the poetic tradition and modern structuralists explan it with intertextuality which refers to the layering of other texts within a text.

Another reason why poetry tends to deflect literal meanings and perpetually prods its readers to make new meanings is the fact that some of the words like pronouns (I, you, s/he) and temporal or spatial adverbs like now, here, then, there have shifting referents. The process of making meaning becomes doubly difficult for poetic images which can be both fictional and real, also at times, atemporal and ahistorical. The poet makes no direct reference to time, event or persons involved. The reader has to match the descriptions of the

scene with the events he knows to bring coherence to the verse. These events can be social, political, literary or historical about the times of the poet or of others. Try to figure out the referents of personal pronouns in the following Ghalib couplet
main unhen chhedun aur kuchh n kahen
chal nikalate jo mai piye hote
I provoke him and he doesn't say anything
He would have walked away if he was drunk

Or the adverbial (*vahan*) in the following famous lines of Shailendra from the film *Guide*
Vahan kaun hai tera, musafir, jaayega kahan
dam lele ghadi bhar, ye chhaiyan, paayega kahan
Who is there for you, traveller, why go there
Rest a while, you won't get this shade anywhere

The hallmark of reading poetry is that the reader as much enjoys this game of solving the poetic puzzle as the poet rejoices in making it. That is why poets deliberately or for other reasons like economy or aesthetics introduce ambiguity or silences in their texts. Take for example Firaq Gorakhpuri's couplet
Iqaraar-e-gunah-e-ishq sun lo
mujh se ik baat ho gayee hai
Let me confess in love a sin
As it is, I have done a thing
The stanza neither tells the reader the 'sin' nor explains the 'thing', so what kind of a 'confession' it is. Despite this, it is one of the most popular and often quoted couplets. Similarly, see what Nasir Kazmi says
raat bhar ham na so sake 'nasir'
parda-e-khamoshi men kya kuchh tha
I could not sleep the whole night 'Nasir'
The dark cover of silence had a lot in it (61.7)

The reader does not know what the 'cover of silence' had in it, even when it was 'a lot'. Moreover, the pronoun 'hum' can refer to both singular and plural noun; choosing one against the other in this case can make a lot of difference in meaning. This vagueness is both a challenge and an enterprise for the reader. It compels the reader to engage in a dialogue with the poet and reach at some kind of an agreement. The economy of phrasing without giving any clear or full explanation is in fact a poetic signal for readers to open up their minds, eyes and ears and experience the unsaid. These silences or gaps are the beauty spots of poetry and thrive on the emotional uncertainties, and undefined longings of the reader. When people say that poetry is timeless, it is primarily because of these qualities. A master poet will deploy them to high advantage and carry his readers along with him and lead them to pleasures or spectacles yet not imagined or experienced.

Ghazals of Nasir

Nasir's poetry is no exception. It has all of these qualities, that is why it has withstood the test of time and is still appreciated and critically acclaimed. He blends the best of poetic practices with his personal history and the history of his time, yet gives it a texture that is both lyrically romantic and emotionally impersonal.

It is pertinent here to say a few words about the structure of the genre of ghazal. It is a unique form of poetry in which unlike any other form, we rarely see thematic unity. The number of stanzas in a ghazal may vary from five to fifteen (or more), all with varying topics; the only unity it is compelled to have is that of rhyme and meter. Each stanza comprises two lines, usually called a couplet. Barring the initial couplet whose two lines must rhyme with each other, the rest of the couplets are somewhat free relatively. They often have their first line open-ended, but the second line again strictly conforms to the rhyme scheme set in the first couplet. In fact, the initial couplet of the ghazal sets the tone and the rhyme of the ghazal which each of the subsequent couplet is obliged to follow in the second line.

The metrical and rhythmic unity is the sole criterion that keeps all the units of a ghazal together, otherwise, each couplet is free to explore new areas of thought, emotion and mood. In most of the ghazals, unlike a nazm, we do not have a theme uniformly sustained in all of its stanzas. However, it is not the norm. There are instances of many ghazals by eminent poets where a certain idea or an emotion rules over the entire composition and gives it a thematic or emotional unity. But such ghazals are not common and it is left to the ingenuity of the reader to perceive that hidden unity.

Nasir Kazmi also presents the same kaleidoscopic pattern in his ghazals. Notwithstanding, the features of ambiguity, as given above, his verses betray a wide variety of themes and emotions. The beauty of his poetry enhances manifold when we read them in the background of his personal life and experience. His ghazals may seem like speaking of his own pleasures or pains, as some times they are in first person, yet on second reading, they turn out to be representative images of the generation that has seen waxing and waning forms of love, historical upheavals and massive material, emotional and spiritual loss. Ghazal which usually addresses a theme of love undergoes an enormous change at the hands of Nasir Kazmi. The otherworldliness, a staple of the traditional poetry, at times becomes a mere luxury of imagination with him, an unattainable quantity that distracts us from the grim realities of this world.
zindagi ke azaab kya kam hain
kyun gham-e-lamakan kare koyi
As if there are fewer troubles in this life
Why add more of the other-life, uninvited *(50.3)*
With a heavy slant towards reality and public concerns, his poetry becomes the voice of a million hearts. This is what puts him in the front row of modern ghazal poets and gets him to be counted as one of its pioneers.

I will like to take up Ghazal 9 for illustration of some of the major themes on which Nasir Kazmi spends his energies.

9.1
basa huya hai khayalon men koyi paikar-e-naaz
bula rahi hai abhi tak vo dilnashin awaaz
Someone of a gentle bearing occupies my mind
That impelling voice keeps calling me from behind

The *matlaa* of the ghazal is a typical love couplet with the ambiguity, of course, about who that 'someone of a gentle bearing" is. Nevertheless, it clearly refers to the love that has been lost or abandoned. Most of Nasir's poetry, as we shall read, deals with the 'post-love' condition. His lexicon is romantic, at times folksy and prosaic though, it speaks less of romance than it sounds..

LOVE: Whatever romance we find in his verses is in the form of 'love' that once was. We will rarely find him in the middle of an amorous relationship or expressing his ardent love in the present time. Take another one
yaad aata hai roz-o-shab koyi
ham se rootha hai besabab koyi
I long to see someone night and day
Who for no reason just turned away (93.1)
In another example he has even lost the memory of that old love
kabhi kabhi jo tere qurb men guzare the
ab un dinon ka tasavvur bhi mere paas nahin
The few moments close to you that I spent
Are gone forever leaving no trace or scent *(90.4)*

Sometimes, he seems like speaking to his beloved in the present time, but the tone is still of doubt and despair
dikhaun dagh-e-mohabbat jo nagavaar na ho
sunaun qissa-e-furqat agar bura na lage
I can show scars of love, if it is not unkind
Tell tales of our parting if you don't mind *(91.4)*

Traditional love based on appreciation of beauty and intense emotions is rare in his poetry. In fact, romance is a lost metaphor and Nasir left anchorless in the new age, laments its receding power. Separation, distance, unfulfilled desire are the usual themes he prefers to deal with.
ye bhi hai ek tarah ki mohabbat
main tujh se tu mujh se juda hai
It is a love story of a different sort
I from you, you from me live apart *(52.8)*

In fact, sometimes he goes to the other extreme and dismisses love as something insignificant
juda hue hain bahut log ek tum bhi sahi
ab itni baat pe kya zindagi haraam karen
So many have deserted, let you be one of them
For this alone I will not let my life to grieving *(89.5)*

NOSTALGIA: At another level couplet 9.1 is highly symbolic of nostalgia — of things, places and people that are lost or left behind. Nasir migrated to Pakistan in 1947. He had spent the best of his young years in India — his father had a farm in Ambala where he also used to work. The memory of those days haunts him, surfaces in his poetry again and again one way or the other. In this verse, he can hear the call of someone he was fond of. A similar feeling in another one
ek anokhee basti dhyaan men basati hai
us basti ke baasi mujhe bulaate hain
A strange community lives in my head
Its inhabitants keep calling me over *(26.2)*

In other verses, he also recalls the happy times he spent in the past
raunaqen theen jahan men kya kya kuchh
log the raftagaan men kya kya kuchh
What joyous times this world had, imagine
What wonderful souls once we had, imagine (72.1)
But most of the time he misses the people and places, and regrets the loss that has resulted from that dislocation
mushkil hai fir milen kabhi yaarane-raftagan
taqdeer hi se ab ye karamaat ho to ho
Little hope, lost friends will ever meet again
It will be but a miracle of luck, if at all (10.2)

Ghazals like 26 and 39 are mainly given to this feeling of nostalgia, loss and pain. He not only misses those old people, some of them dead by then, but also obliquely makes a reference to his old associations back in India

kyun na roun teri judaai men
din guzaare hain tere paas bahut
Why should I not cry on parting
What good days we had in life (40.3)

He is full of appreciation and love for those old folks and places. These poems are elegiac in tone and show reverence towards the old generation who were more affectionate, sensitive and tolerant. In the same nostalgic tone, he also regrets the loss of those who were torch bearers to the society but have now been consumed by death.

zindagi jin ke tasavvur se jila paati thi
haaye kya log the jo daam-e-ajal men aaye
Reminiscing about them alone brings to life shine
What amazing people who fell to the trap of time (98.5)

9.2
vahi dinon men tapish hai vahi shabon men gudaaz
magar ye kya ki meri zindagi men soz na saaz
Days have same warmth, nights the same vigour
But in my life there is neither grief nor pleasure

This second couplet points towards poet's state of mental vacuity or possibly his restlessness, despite the calm and ordinariness around him. In fact, this external calm is deceptive as it gives him neither pleasure nor pain. More than everyday cycle of life, the couplet foregrounds his inner turmoil or something that keeps nagging his heart. And it is not only in this verse, it is all over his poetry.

RESTLESSNESS: The eternally restive mind of Nasir is the bedrock on which rests most of his poetic realm. Most of the times, this restlessness, this melancholy remains undefined and without any obvious reasons.

aaj to be-sabab udaas hai ji
ishq hota to koyi baat bhi thi
Heart feels sad today for no good reason
If love it were, I'd have some consolation (1.1)

Though his sadness is unexplained, but the present couplet suggests a certain lack or loss of love. We can also read in many parts of his poetry repeated references to deprivation, lovelessness and loneliness
be-kaif be-nishat na thi is qadar hayat
jeena agarche ishq men aasan na tha kabhi
Life was never so dismal, unpleasant as it is now
Though it was never easy under the vows of love (51.8)
kaun is raah se guzarta hai
dil yun hi intizar karta hai
Who, I guess, will pass by this lane
The heart though waits in vain *(42.1)*

Loneliness is a recurrent theme in Nasir's poetry. He was not a loner, but a proper friendly person. Yet his poetry abounds in its reference as it is this state of mind in which he engages his poetic muse.
akele ghar se puchhti hai bekasi
tera diya jalaane vaale kya huye
Misery that dwells in the lonely house asks
Those who kept it lighted, where are they (92.7)

Absence of love or continuance of sorrow, personal or of others, may not necessarily do the explanation. At best, it may suggest a certain rankling in his mind that was spurred probably by the state of affairs he had witnessed. But restlessness was a general state of Nasir's mind
jab koyi gham nahin hota 'nasir'
bekali dil ka siva hoti hai
When 'Nasir' has no sorrows
An agitated heart is what he is (35.13)

QUEST: In fact, restlessness in Nasir is an important source of his creativity. Nasir is a night crawler, a seeker, an explorer, a dreamer, a nature lover and an aspirational chaser who is looking for something.
laakh rahen theen laakh jalwe the
ahd-e-awaargi men kya kuchh tha
Many trails to follow, many marvels to see

The time of free-wheeling had a lot in it (61.2)

Though he would not divulge what exactly he was looking for, yet at times he gives a hint that all he hopes to find is a small happy sign which, he puts ironically, is just an ordinary expectation.
udaas phirta hun main jis ki dhun men barson se
yunhi si hai vo khushi baat vo zara si hai
For years what I have been looking for sadly
Is something trivial - a bit of happiness actually (34.6)
Or
un ujaalon ki dhun men phirta hun
chhab dikhaate hi jo guzar jaayen
I am earnestly looking for those lights
That fade away as soon as they glow (77.4)

But his rambling in the city was not always cut out for creativity. It was a part of his restlessness, not particularly given to any promise.
dil men har waqt chubhan rahti thi
thi mujhe kis ki talab yaad nahin
In my heart I always had an aching urge
What exactly I hungered for, I remember not (73.3)

But, at the bottom of his heart he always had hope that something good would come up
kya khabar khaak hi se koyi kiran phoot pade
zauq-e-awaargi-e-dasht-o-bayaban hi sahi
Who can tell from dust may arise a ray of light
Let me have, in desert and woods, a free flight (27.3)

9.3
na chhed ai khalish-e-dard baar-baar na chhed
chhupaye baitha hoon seene men ek umr ke raaz
O nagging pain, don't try too much my patience
Buried in my heart are old secrets of conscience

Here he admits that he has pain and he does not want it to provoke him too much too often, otherwise he will spill out the old secrets that he has kept hidden in his chest. Now there is no hint to the reader what these secrets are, but sure enough they are painful. Based on inferences drawn from the poet's life and his writings, critics have assumed that these secrets are the terrible wounds that he still nurses after witnessing the gruesome scenes of the Partition.

PARTITION: There are innumerable references in his poetry that subscribe to this tragedy, sometimes in a direct manner.
gali gali abaad thi jin se kahan gaye vo log
dilli ab ke aisi ujadi ghar ghar phaila sog
Who kept the streets abuzz, where are they
The destruction of Delhi has left all in disarray (21.1)

This is how he describes the scenes of violence that were witnessed during the partition movements across the border.
shahr-dar-shahr ghar jalaaye gaye
yun bhi jashn-e-tarab manaaye gaye
Cities after cities, homes were set on fire
That's how festivities were made there (76.1)

If in one place he agonises over physical destruction then in another over massive manslaughter like in the following.
din dahaade ye lahu ki holi
khalq ko khauf khuda ka na raha
In broad daylight, this parade of bloodbath
Do folks have no fear of God or his wrath (74.6)

Again in another, he expresses his outrage at the humiliation that was meted out to women
kyaa kahoon kis tarah sar-e-bazaar
ismaton ke diye bujhaaye gaye
What can I say how in the broad daylight
Honour and dignity were made to despair (76.3)

Besides such direct references, his poems are interspersed with several indirect verses which are equally voluble about his anguish over this human carnage. Ghazals 66 and 84 are such examples
phool khushboo se juda hai ab ke
yaaro ye kaisi hava hai ab ke

Fragrance leaves the flowers this time
What gusty winds, we have this time (66.1)

Take another couplet from another ghazal
dete hain suraagh fasl-e-gul ka
shakhon pe jale hue basere
The charred twigs and nests tell
The harvest of flowers that fell (96.4)

Not only this despicable human destruction, the terrific hardships, the mental trauma and the emotional loss experienced during migration journeys or after are also an integral part of his partition poems. A ghazal like 83 though romantic in tone is one of the best symbolic representations of this partition disaster. One of its most touching couplets is
tu kis khayaal men hai manzilon ke shaidai
unhen bhi dekh jinhen raaste men neend aai
What is it that drives you mad about journey's end
Think of those who went into last sleep on the bend   (83.2)

Notwithstanding this great human tragedy, Nasir, as a sensitive poet, is more concerned about the mental and emotional agonies which he referred above as the secrets of conscience.
itaab-e-ahl-e-jahan sab bhula diye lekin
vo zakhm yaad hain ab tak jo ghayabana lage
I have all forgotten the worldly blows to me
But not the deep hits that lie buried in me (91.8)

9.4
bas ab to ek hi dhun hai ki neend aa jaaye
vo din kahan ki uthayen shab-e-firaq ke naaz
'I want sleep' is now my one and only petition
Gone are days I cherished nights of separation

Nasir claims that he has no time for the sorrows of the night of separation which we know have been the prime event for love poets. A lover would spend the night awake waiting for the beloved and in the process half paralyse himself with fatigue, pain and hopelessness. Nasir, on the contrary, wants to get some sleep on this night. Either he has no beloved now or he has realised its futility in the light of contemporary love; or perhaps, in the quest for new ideas he wants to abandon this trite old romantic trope. We have seen earlier that there is very little in the form of tête-à-tête between two passionate lovers in Nasir's poetry. The other options, thus, cannot entirely be ruled out as Nasir spends a lot of his poetic time referring to *shab-e-firaq*, sometimes in contexts other than the traditional. We shall soon see that in the discussion of other couplets.

Here I would like to illustrate a feature of his poetry that stands out in many of his verses and I call it a 'contest of contraries'. Nasir often chooses to present a lexical combination, an image or a view that includes terms contrary to each other. In the present couplet he presents a position that is contrary to common expectation in love. This stylistic device may have underneath a desire to present an unusual lexical match or to build a new perspective by juxtaposing contraries to dissolve the binaries we generally understand.

CONTRARIES: Look how eagerness or restlessness has been yoked with relief in the following couplet
ai dil kise nasib ye taufeeq-e-iztiraab
milti hai zindagi men ye rahat kabhi kabhi
Not all hearts are worthy of restlessness
Only a few receive this bliss at times (28.2)

Or fierce and quiet
jab zara tez hava hoti hai
kaisi sunsaan faza hoti hai
When there is that fierce wind
How quiet the all-around is (35.1)

In another, he juxtaposes 'chill' and 'fire' (71.2), and then 'river' and 'thirst' (5.9). Again, he calls cool dewdrops 'seething' in 18.8. In a very clever use of both poetic and idiomatic language he brings in a good alliance between sunshine and darkness in 16.3.

Here are some examples where concepts contrary to our general expectations are presented
ye kya ki ek taur se guzre tamaam umr
ji chahta hai ab koyi tere siva bhi ho
What monotony to have the same thing each day
Wish there were someone other than you, I pray *(6.3)*
niyyat-e-shauq bhar na jaye kahin
tu bhi dil se utar na jaye kahin
What if love gets full and fades away
What if the heart too casts you away (62.1)

Such contraries are not off-hand, they are basically representative of a time which was in transition and had seen several reversals of ideas and phenomena. Nasir writes liberally about such changes, but always with a sense of uncertainty and an underlying feeling of loss or regret. Here are some of the images where this transition is obvious, but do mark the contrast.
yun na ghabraye huye phirte the
dil ajab kunj-e-aman tha pahle
Never in the past did I feel so restless
As heart was such a big source of solace (47.6)
ik sada sang men tadpi hogi
ik sharar phool men larza hoga
A cry would have caused a rock to tremor
A fire spark would have lurked in a flower (31.9)

9.5
guzar hi jaayegi ai dost tere hijr ki raat
ki tujhse badh ke tera dard hai mera damsaaz
Mate, this night without you will soon be over
As more than you, this pain is now my partner

Despite his wish for a sleepful night (9.4) he is not sure whether he will have one, but assures his departed friend that he will survive the night anyhow, as the pain that she has given has become his real comforter. As usual, it is not clear who this friend is but the couplet foregrounds not the friend but the significance of night, especially the night of separation and the intensity of pain that the speaker

experiences. This pain or grief remains a constant feature in Nasir's poetry and can be interpreted variously in different contexts.
saaye ki tarah mere saath rahe ranj-o-alam
gardish-e-waqt kahin raas na aayi mujh ko
Worries and woes followed me like a shadow
The cycle of time did I never learn to follow (7.5)

NIGHT OF SEPARATION: How important the night is or how promising his nightly sojourn into the city was has already been mentioned. A solitary night or a night of separation and pain, which mostly turns into an act of self reflection, has produced some of the finest verses in Nasir. It is that time of his waking hours when his mind is on a poetic overdrive.
Jab raat gaye teri yaad aayi so tarah se jee ko behlaaya
Kabhi apne hi dil se baaten ki kabhi teri yaad ko samjhaaya
At night, missing you, I tried to amuse my heart
Talked to it at times, consoled my memory in part (not included)

Night of separation takes different shades depending upon the mood of the poet. If it is extreme pain in couplet 9.5 then it is plain emptiness in the following
mahroom-e-khwab dida-e-hairan na tha kabhi
tera ye rang ai shab-e-hijran na tha kabhi
My curious eyes were never so bereft of dreams
Nor was the lonely night ever so dull, it seems (51.1)

At the same time, it is all pleasure in the following
tere firaq ki raaten kabhi na bhulengi
maze mile unhin raaton men umr bhar ke mujhe
Never will I forget the nights of your separation
They gave pleasure indeed of a lifetime to me (46.5)

And a state of partial torpor in the following
ojhal huye jaate hain nigaahon se do aalam
tum aaj kahan ho gham-e-furqat ke sahaaro
My vision of both the worlds is getting fuzzy
Where are those who stood by me in misery *(95.5)*

The night, as most often represented in Urdu poetry, is also spent in waiting for love
kahan hai tu ki tere intizar men ai dost
tamaam raat sulagte hain dil ke virane
I Looked for you all night, where are you, mate
The arid corners of my heart burn bright in wait (25.6)

NIGHT: Night by itself is a very prominent motif in the poetry of Nasir. We know its importance in his life, but in his poetry too it figures at regular intervals. Night is a trope that portrays his poetic mindset and stands for a variety of emotions and interests.
dhyaan ki sidhiyon pe pichhle pahar
koyi chupke se paanv dharta hai
In the late hours of a brooding night
Someone moves in with a step light (42.4)

Night is the most meditative and creative time for Nasir. See how night signifies his creativity
gulshan-e-fikr ki munh-band kali
shab-e-mahtab men va hoti hai
A budding idea in mind's garden
Opens up when moonlit the night is (35.9)

Some of his most popular, to me most romantic and metaphorical couplets, have also come with reference to night.
rain andheri hai aur kinaara door
chand nikle to paar utar jaayen
The night is dark and far is the coast
We can make it if the moon shows up now (77.5)
shab ki tanhaiyon men pichhle pahar
chand karta hai guftugoo ham se
In the late hours of a solitary night
The moon gets to talking with us (36.5)

9.6
ye aur baat ki duniyaa na sun saki varna
sukoot-e-ahl-e-nazar hai baja-e-khud awaaz

It is another matter the world did not listen to it
But the silence of the far-sighted had a voice in it

This couplet deviates from the romantic tone and speaks about those who are wise and silent. The poet cautions the world that though they never could hear them but their silence was a call by itself. Again we cannot figure out who these *ahl-e-nazar* are but with their reference, the verse definitely assumes a political tenor. It warns the people against the maddening noises and urges them to listen to the sane voices. It may be a political pointer to the insanity that people demonstrated during the partition or the general state of chaos in post-independence times where voices of the sensible people got suppressed.

APPEAL: Poets are the unacknowledged legislators of the world, as Shelley says. In their poetic zeal and concern for humanity they do sometimes represent the sane voices in the form of appeals, advice and observations that may make people think. Nasir too in his poems in many places inserted such nuggets of wisdom. Here are some examples in the form of advice
husn ko dil men chhupa kar dekho
dhyan ki shama jala kar dekho
Keep secrets of beauty in your heart
Keep high the flame of your thought (29.1)
jo ghar ujad gaye un ka na ranj kar pyare
vo chara kar ki ye gulshan ujaad sa na lage
Don't bother for nests that were wrecked
Make sure this garden does not get ravaged (91.7)

These verses are phrased in a manner that they can become metaphors for different contexts, though the second couplet above seems clearly politically motivated. The following seems to point towards communal harmony
isi goshe men hain sab dair-o-haram
dil sanam hai ki khuda ghaur se sun
Lodged in this nook is a temple, a mosque
Is your heart an idol or God, listen with care (75.9)

Some pieces of wisdom in Nasir's poetry come in the form of observations and poetic images with high metaphorical content
fakhta chup hai badi der se kyun
sarv ki shakh hila kar dekho
The dove for long is sitting quiet
Give the tree a shake to know why (29.3)
hadsa hai ki khizan se pahle
boo-e-gul gul se juda hoti hai
Before autumn, the fragrance
Leaves the flower, how tragic it is (35.11)

One of the qualities of good leaders or those with a farsight is that they hold on to hope and keep encouraging people to do their best. Nasir presents many instances where he tries to instil hope in his people
shahr ujde to kya hai kushaada zamin-e-khuda
ik naya ghar banayenge ham sabr kar sabr kar
Cities are wrecked, yet there's land of God's plenty
We'll make another, a new home, keep patience (69.5)
phir kisi subah-e-tarab ka jaadu
parda-e-shab se huvaida hoga
A sudden magic of a morning full of delight
Will rise up from behind the curtain of a night (31.8)

9.7
ye besabab naheen shaam-o-sahar ke hangamen
utha raha hai koyi parda-ha-e-raaz-o-niyaaz
Not for nothing have we this day-night strife
Someone is raising curtain on the mystery of life

This is a complex verse. The keyword is '*hangame*'. Does he call the humdrum cycle of day and night 'strife' or is it the social or political upheaval that occupies our days and nights? Equally ambiguous is the term *raaz-o-niyaz*. Is it a reference to the secrets of love or is it about the mystery of the world? The turmoils of the day, especially of those violent days around the partition, could raise questions about the ways of the world or the efficacy of spiritual beliefs. At the same time, the daily engagements with mundane chores could also take away the romance from that proverbial love. In either case the couplet raises a doubt about the sanctity of traditional values both in love and faith due to worldly pressures.

CHANGE: Nasir was acutely conscious of it, that is why his poetry marks a new trend and does not accord the same respect to the traditional sentiments in ghazal. In the following couplet he speaks about the fading intensity of love and possibly the loss of other contingent sentiments like faith and spirituality
sar men jab ishq ka sauda na raha
kya kahen zeest men kya kya na raha
When the madness of love in me left
Can't tell what else in life with it left (74.1)

Couplets of this kind abound in his poetry. They may reflect the general frame of mind and attitude of the people towards traditional ways of life. The pressures of daily life perhaps brought major changes in their life and made them more materialistic.
zindagi ke azaab kya kam hain
kyun gham-e-lamakan kare koyi
As if there are fewer troubles in this life
Why add more of the other-life, uninvited (50.3)

These couplets should not mean Nasir becomes completely oblivious of the spiritual side of life. No, it only means that his concerns in poetry are more given to the real world than the ideal or platonic that we used to find in traditional poetry.
ye bhi araaish-e-hasti ka taqaaza tha ki ham
halqa-e-fikr se maidan-e-amal men aaye
This too was the demand of the celebration of life
That we moved from the abstract to practical life (98.3)

In several verses he expresses his disapproval of traditional thinking or of his contemporaries who continued to do the same hackneyed work.
gar ehtiram-e-rasm-e-wafa hai to ai khuda
ye ehtiram-e-rasm-e-kohan mujh se chheen le
If there is some honour in following a tradition

Then O God! Free me from this old convention 56.2)
Bane banaye hue raston pe jaa nikle
ye hamsafar mere kitne gurez-paa nikle
They took the path that was much travelled
My friends turned out to be wary and laggard (8.1)

What we call modern thinking, which was largely the outcome of the hard times like wars, natural disasters or political changeovers, had brought about a major change in people's perspective on things. Possibly, they had turned more pragmatic and individualistic. This changed mood is what compels the poet to write in a tone different from the earlier. But one cannot miss the irony in it.
khulus-o-mehr-o-wafa log kar chuke hain bahut
mere khayal men ab aur koyi kaam karen
Enough of love, grace, sincerity, we have had
It is time now, besides that, we do something (89.2)

9.8
tera khayal bhi teri tarah mukammal hai
vahi shabab vahi dilkashi vahi andaaz
A thought of you is as wholesome as you are
The same beauty, same charm, same glamour

This can be directly interpreted as a love jingle, yet again, we can see the absence of the beloved. Nasir can conceive of love or the beauty of the beloved in the most enchanting terms but rarely makes it a live and mutually fulfilling affair. Love is most pleasurable but it is always a matter of the past. The beloved is present only in the mind.

At another level, explicating the reference of '*tera*' can transport this couplet to the level of a Sufi refrain.

METAPHYSICAL : As we understand, all love poetry, especially the traditional Urdu, can be interpreted both at the physical and metaphysical level. Sufi streaks of thought are rampant in the love yarns that our classical poets wove around the theme of love. One of the most facilitating elements in the Urdu poetry that allows love songs to be understood at two levels is the general use of masculine gender for the other person or beloved. In this couplet too, 'you' can refer both to the worldly beloved as well as to the ultimate lover that is divine. Nasir's poetry also has its share of romantic as well as metaphysical inferences.

Read the following couplets which are stark romantic in tone but can easily fit into the metaphysical context
tere khayaal se lo de uthi hai tanhai
shab-e-firaq hai ya teri jalwa aarai
A flashback of you has lit up my solitary existence
Is it a lonely night or a celebration of your presence (83.1)
zindagi jis ki tamanna men kati
wo mere haal se begaana raha
All my life I longed for one in desperation
Who remained stranger to my emotion (74.4)

Within the romantic mode, Nasir has also expressed one of the most mystical ideas of Sufism
shuaan-e-husn tere husn ko chhupaati thi
vo roshani thi ki soorat nazar na aati thi
Glowing rays of beauty veiled your visage
Radiance was too much to see your image 78.1)

Besides love songs, there are also other verses where some popular concepts of Sufism have been articulated in the easiest and most beautiful way.
tujh bin saari umr guzari
log kahenge tu mera tha
All my life I lived without you
They say you lived in my abode (54.6)
mahsoos jo hota hai dikhai nahin deta
dil aur nazar men had-e-faazil to vahi hai
What is felt is not always what can be seen
The gap between heart and eye is the same (64.3)

Of course, his most famous *hamd* like ghazal made immortal by Nusrat Fateh Ali khan is

gham hai ya khushi hai tu
meri zindagi hai tu
Grief or joy, what are you
Though life of me are you (24.1)

9.9
sharab-o-sher ki duniya badal gayi lekin
vo aankh dhoondh hi leti hai bekhudi ka javaaz
The realms of wine and verse have changed, yet
The eye can find other ways to swing and forget

This is a couplet about the art of poetry, its substance and its process. In consonance with his poetry, Nasir agrees that the world of poetry has undergone a change. Just as people have found new ways to get drunk, the poets too have found new ways to get besotted with poetry. In short, if love is not the theme to turn the heads of the poet then they will find other subjects to get on to their poetic high. It is a significant couplet in the light of the new poetry that many critics think was introduced by such modern poets as Nasir Kazmi. About his inability to write about traditional themes like love, nasir, making an allusion to Farhad, confesses
na shaghl-e-khara-tarashi na karobaar-e-junoon
main koh-o-dasht men faryad-o-naala kya karta
When I am neither in mad love nor rock-felling
Then why on a mountain shall I pray by yelling (68.3)

NEW POETRY: One of the highlights of the new poetry was that it was socially conscious. The metaphors of love which were until then being used at two levels, physical and metaphysical, were now being turned around to take on the political dimension. *Burg e nai* was published in 1952 and it already had a substantial coverage given to the partition, migration and its aftermath. Nasir's later writings also had an equal measure of political poetry as it depicted and criticised the social and political developments in his country. Unlike Faiz Ahmed Faiz or Sahir Ludhianvi or other progressive poets, Nasir did not wear his political ideology or affiliation on his sleeve. He remained concerned in his cool melancholic way to describe the injustice to people and callousness of the authorities. Whereas other socially conscious poets took refuge in nazm as their vehicle of protest, Nasir continued with the ghazal genre and gave it a new feel.

A ghazal like 11 is a good introduction to the kind of political views he would express in a number of poems. Ruling coterie of the rich, country's economic dependence on others, appalling condition of its poor are some of the themes that came under Nasir's pen
chand gharaanon ne mil-jul kar
kitne gharon ka haq chheena hai
A few families with their joint might
Robbed many a home of their right (11.1)

In other ghazals, he is making reference to the oppressive regime that his country saw post-independence
koyi to haq-shanaas ho ya rab
zulm ko naravaa kahe koyi
O god, someone must speak up for rights
And 'repression is not right' dare say (39.6)

Ghazal 41 is a true poetic endeavor to represent the state of affairs of his country during those despotic times. Unlike the above examples where he directly expresses his protest, this is a ghazal that is highly metaphorical and makes the best use of poetic gestures and indirections.
kaarvan sust rahbar khamosh
kaise guzrega ye safar khamosh
Caravan sluggish, the guide in silence
How'd we make this journey in silence (41.1)

At times, Nasir also gets carried and speaks in the language of revolution.
ye mahallat-e-shahi tabaahi ke hain muntazir
girne vaale hain un ke alam sabr kar sabr kar
These royal palaces are waiting to be demolished
We will see their flags go down, keep patience (69.6)
badal sako to badal do ye baghbaan varna
ye baagh saya-e-sarv-o-saman ko tarsega

You must change the gardener, if you can, else
The garden will miss shade of flowers and a tree (99.5)

Besides socio-political themes like the partition or civil disorders, Nasir also often speaks about 'transition' and change. These are broader themes which we have already discussed under nostalgia, restlessness, and impatience with tradition. His perception of change is not always laced with regret; it is also at times bound with hope and progress
har nafas shauq bhi hai manzil ka
har qadam yaad-e-raftagan bhi hai
Every breath is a step towards the goal
Yet it is a reminder of the past too (19.7)

NATURE: The other important theme that moves Nasir's poetic muse is nature. By his own admission, Nasir was a man of nature. We have therefore abundant references to nature in his poetry. Most of them have been metaphorically used to express various moods. Look at the following with reference to the old generation.
ham jis ped ki chhaanv men baitha karate the
ab us ped ke patte jhadte jaate hain
The shade tree we use to sit under
Is now shedding its leaves all over (26.1)

But, besides this poetic use, he has also written a number of ghazals where he directly shows his love for nature.
kunj-kunj nagmazan basant aa gayi
ab sajegi anjuman basant aa gayi
Arrived in every corner is the melody of spring
Festive will be our gatherings now with spring (not included)

Pehli Barish, his long poem on a single rhyme is full of such beautiful images which celebrate nature
tere angan ke pichhvade
sabz darakhton ka ramna tha
At the back of your courtyard
Trees made a cool green holt (100.8)

Nasir has also composed a number of verses where he shows his concern for the conservation of nature. It is amazing to know that he could foresee its importance in his time. Here he refers to the drying rivers.
sunaata hai koyi bhooli kahaani
mahakte mithe dariyaon ka paani
Someone tells a tale long lost
Of rivers and waters sweet most (80.1)

And here to the loss of woods
sahme-sahme the raat ahl-e-chaman
tha koyi aadami darakhaton men
Inmates of the woods were alarmed
A man in dark was lurking in the trees (20.12)

9.10
urooj par hai mera dard in dinon 'nasir'
meri gazal men dhadkati hai vaqt ki awaaz
These days 'Nasir' the anguish in me is at its prime
At the heart of my ghazal beats the call of the time

This may be considered as the poet's self-proclamation about his work. When his pain, his melancholy, his distress gets too intense, it translates into a ghazal that sings to the heartbeat of the public of his time. In other words, Nasir's poetry though romantic and nostalgic at times is essentially supposed to be a representation of the times he lived. There is not much to argue with Nasir on this claim. In another ghazal, he writes
saare is daur ki munh bolti tasveeren hain
koyi dekhe mere deewan ke kirdaaron ko
All of them are well-known portraits of our times
If you take a look at my anthology of characters (97.5)

PEOPLE'S POET: Though Nasir has written a lot of love poetry yet his love is not merely interpersonal; it is also for the people, their grievances, their suffering. We have already seen samples of his poetry where he has shown his angst again the inhuman atrocities that were committed during his time. We have also read how sometimes he goes a step further and takes a swipe at the leaders and their misdemeanour. Nasir seems to be consciously working in his poetry to make it a vehicle for articulating the silent voices of his people. The grieving, the suffering or the oppressed public in an

undemocratic set up rarely find a platform where they can speak out. That is why Nasir claims
ham ne bakhshi hai khamoshi ko zaban
dard majboor-e-fughan tha pahle
We have bestowed speech to silence
Pain depended solely on crying once   (47.14)

There are repeated references to silence in his poetry which represents the suppression of freedom and complete subjugation of the masses.
ye khamoshi to rag-o-pai men rach gayi 'nasir'
vo naala kar ki dil-e-sang se sadaa nikle
This silence has settled deep in your gut 'Nasir'
Bewail so loud that even a stone heart will stir   (8.5)

Nasir has particularly a soft corner for the poor and the utterly disadvantaged, as at several places he speaks of nurturing them.
khuda agar kabhi kuchh ikhtiyaar de ham ko
tu pahle khak-nashinon ka intizaam karen
If God ever grants me some control over things
To the lowly ones, I will first provide something   (89.6)

But he cannot help them much, as he says apologetically, except by his poetic endeavours
yahi sher hain meri saltanat isi fan men hai mujhe aafiyat
mere kasa-e-shab-o-roz men tere kaam ki koyi shai nahin
My verses are my estate, my joy too,
with this art alone I make do
What I have in my bowl from day and night
is hardly of any use to you   (87.7)

There are also references where he accuses his contemporaries of not showing the same sensitivity towards those public grievances (87). At the same time he knows the impact of poetry; and fears persecution like some other poets of his time had to face.
gul-rez meri nala-kashi se hai shakh shakh
gulchin ka bas chale to ye fan mujh se chhin le
With my cries, I make every bough cast flowers
Left to the florist, he will strip me of my powers   (56.4)

Like all poets who call for humanism, equality and justice, he also deplored class divisions in his country and advocated equal rights for all

ye khas-o-aam ki bekar guftugu kab tak
qubool ki jiye jo faisla awaam karen
Why have this futile debate on high and low
Let us accept what comes as people's ruling   (89.3)

Nasir, like some other socially awakened poets, could only speak for a limited time and on a few of those social ills. The world is too big and full of too many struggles for the comman man. No one can do enough to do justice to them. That is why he is conscious of his or any poet's piecemeal efforts at social writing.
hikayat-e-gham-e-duniya ko chahiye daftar
varaq varaq mere dil ka risaala kya karta
The story of the worldly woes needs a full office
A few pages of my heart's journal won't suffice   (68.4)

Nasir was aware of his popularity among masses. For him emotional intensity and poetic effect is more important than other things. That is why he keeps his poetry free from poetic clutter and close to the ordinary readers
har aadmi nahin shaista-e-rumooz-e-sukhan
vo kamsukhan ho mukhatab to hamkalaam karen
Not all are familiar with subtleties of poetry
With a less articulate, we choose speaking   *(89.4)*

Poets are not warrior in the true sense but are known for wielding their pen to fight, protest and stand for values like freedom and justice. The world has a long history of such writers. It is difficult to assess how much impact their writings make on the ways of the world, but the world would be a poorer place if it did not have these paper crusaders. Every generation will need a new set of these imaginative thinkers; the journey of their crusade knows no end.

Ghazal 23, a sort of self-obituary by Nasir Kazmi, reiterates this and many other emotions that we discussd earlier. To end, we can say as he says in this poem - May this 'nightly rambler', this 'star performer' 'stay alive forever'.

1. *aaj to be-sabab udaas hai jee*

aaj to be-sabab udaas hai ji
ishq hota to koyi baat bhi thi
jalta phirta hun main dopahron men
jaane kya cheez kho gayi meri
vahin phirta hun main bhi khak-basar
is bhare shahr men hai ek gali
chhupta phirta hai ishq duniya se
phailti ja rahi hai rusvai (4)
ham-nashin kya kahun ki vo kya hai
chhod ye baat neend udne lagi
aaj to vo bhi kuchh khamosh sa tha
main ne bhi us se koyi baat na ki
ek dam us ke hont choom liye
ye mujhe baithe baithe kya sujhi
ek dam us ka haath chhod diya
jaane kya baat darmiyan aayi (8)
tu jo itna udaas hai 'nasir'
tujhe kya ho gaya bata to sahi

आज तो बे-सबब उदास है जी
इश्क़ होता तो कोई बात भी थी
जलता फिरता हूँ मैं दोपहरों में
जाने क्या चीज़ खो गई मेरी
वहीं फिरता हूँ मैं भी ख़ाक-बसर
इस भरे शहर में है एक गली
छुपता फिरता है इश्क़ दुनिया से
फैलती जा रही है रुस्वाई (4)
हम-नशीं क्या कहूँ कि वो क्या है
छोड़ ये बात नींद उड़ने लगी
आज तो वो भी कुछ ख़मोश सा था
मैं ने भी उस से कोई बात न की
एक दम उस के होंट चूम लिए
ये मुझे बैठे बैठे क्या सूझी
एक दम उस का हाथ छोड़ दिया
जाने क्या बात दरमियाँ आई (8)
तू जो इतना उदास है 'नासिर'
तुझे क्या हो गया बता तो सही

1. Heart feels sad today for no good reason

Heart feels sad today for no good reason
If love it were, I'd have some consolation

I ramble around on hot afternoons
Have I lost something or someone?

Like others, I go about raising dust
In that one street of this bustling town

Love is hiding itself from the world
Spread all around is mortification (4)

What can I say, my friend, what she is
Forget her, to my sleep it's a disruption

Today, a little quiet she seemed
I too did not speak much or question

On an impulse, I kissed her on the lips
Not knowing what drove my intention

Suddenly, my hand slipped out of hers
Something came up in our conversation (8)

That you are heavy-hearted 'Nasir'
What has happened, tell me the reason

2. aaj tujhe kyun chup si lagi hai

aaj tujhe kyun chup si lagi hai
kuchh to bata kya baat huyi hai
aaj to jaise saari duniya
ham dono ko dekh rahi hai
tu hai aur be-khwab dariche
main hun aur sunsan gali hai
khair tujhe to jaana hi tha
jaan bhi tere saath chali hai (4)
ab to aankh laga le 'nasir'
dekh to kitni raat gayi hai

आज तुझे क्यूँ चुप सी लगी है
कुछ तो बता क्या बात हुई है
आज तो जैसे सारी दुनिया
हम दोनों को देख रही है
तू है और बे-ख़्वाब दरीचे
मैं हूँ और सुनसान गली है
ख़ैर तुझे तो जाना ही था
जान भी तेरे साथ चली है (4)
अब तो आँख लगा ले 'नासिर'
देख तो कितनी रात गई है

2. Why are you sunk in silence so deep

Why are you sunk in silence so deep
What is it, tell me something please

It looks like the entire world today
Has seized us in their gaze

It is you and the undreaming windows
It is me and these deserted alleys

I know, you were anyway bound to go
With you too my zest for life leaves (4)

Close your eyes and sleep now 'Nasir'
The night has seen much of your unease

3. *ab un se aur taqaza-e-baada kya karta*

ab un se aur taqaza-e-baada kya karta
jo mil gaya hai main us se ziyaada kya karta
bhala huya ki tere raste ki khaak huya
main ye taveel safar pa-piyaada kya karta
musafiron ki to khair apni apni manzil thi
teri gali ko na jaata to jaada kya karta
tujhe to ghere hi rahte hain rang rang ke log
tere huzoor mera harf-e-saada kya karta (4)
bas ek chehra kitabi nazar men hai 'nasir'
kisi kitab se main istifaada kya karta

अब उन से और तक़ाज़ा-ए-बादा क्या करता
जो मिल गया है मैं उस से ज़ियादा क्या करता
भला हुआ कि तिरे रास्ते की ख़ाक हुआ
मैं ये तवील सफ़र पा-पियादा क्या करता
मुसाफ़िरों की तो ख़ैर अपनी अपनी मंज़िल थी
तिरी गली को न जाता तो जादा क्या करता
तुझे तो घेरे ही रहते हैं रंग रंग के लोग
तिरे हुज़ूर मिरा हर्फ़-ए-सादा क्या करता (4)
बस एक चेहरा किताबी नज़र में है 'नासिर'
किसी किताब से मैं इस्तिफ़ादा क्या करता

3. More of this wine I wouldn't ask for me

More of this wine I wouldn't ask for me
It serves me enough, what I have got for me

Blessed I was to turn into dust on your way
How else could I foot over this long way

When other travellers had their ways to go
I had only one, and it was you for me to go

Dazzling crowds always hover around you
How could my words become sound for you

I see a face 'Nasir' that reads like a book
What else is there to gain from another book

4. *ai hamsukhan wafa ka taqaaza hai ab yahi*

ai hamsukhan wafa ka taqaaza hai ab yahi
main apne haath kaat loon, tu apne honth si
kin bedilon men fenk diya hadisaat ne
aankhon men jin ke noor na baaton men taazgi
bol ai mere dayaar ki soyi huyi zamin
main jin ko dhoondhata hoon kahan hain vo aadmi
vo shaayaron ka shahr vo Lahore bujh gaya
ugate the jis men sher vo kheti hi jal gayi (4)
meethe the jin ke fal vo shajar kat-kata gaye
thandi thi jis ki chhaanv vo deewar gir gayi
bazaar band, raaste sunsaan, bechiraag
vo raat hai ki ghar se nikalata nahin koyi

ऐ हमसुख़न वफ़ा का तक़ाज़ा है अब यही
मैं अपने हाथ काट लूँ तू अपने होंठ सी
किन बेदिलों में फेंक दिया हादिसात ने
आँखों में जिनकी नूर न बातों में ताज़गी
बोल ऐ मिरे दयार की सोई हुई ज़मीं
मैं जिनको ढूँढ़ता हूँ कहाँ हैं वो आदमी
वो शायरों का शहर वो लाहौर बुझ गया
उगते थे जिसमें शेर वो खेती ही जल गयी (4)
मीठे थे जिनके फल वो शजर कट-कटा गये
ठण्डी थी जिसकी छाँव वो दीवार गिर गयी
बाज़ार बन्द, रास्ते सुनसान, बेचिराग़
वो रात है कि घर से निकलता नहीं कोई

--continue--

4. Friends, loyalty now has for us new scripts

Friends, loyalty now has for us new scripts
I chop off my hands, you seal your lips

Misfortunes landed us with such unkind folks
Who have neither vision, nor vigour in talks

Awake now, the sleeping soil of my land
Where are they - the people I hope to find

The city of poets, Lahore's fire snuffed out
Its harvest, the crop of verses, burnt out (4)

Trees that bore sweet fruit have been hacked
The wall that offered cool shade has collapsed

Markets locked, streets deserted and unlighted
It is a night, no one out of home can be sighted
                              --continue--

4. ai hamsukhan wafa ka taqaaza hai ab yahi

galiyon men ab to shaam se firte hain pahredar
hai koyi-koyi shama so vo bhi bujhi-bujhi
ai roshani-e-deeda-o-dil ab nazar bhi aa
duniyaa tere firaaq men andher ho gayi (8)
alqissa jeb chaak hi karani padi hamen
go ibtidaa-e-gham men badi ehatiyaat ki
ab jee men hai ki sar kisi patthar se fodiye
mumkin hai qalb-e-sang se nikale koyi pari
bekaar baithe rahane se behatar hai koyi din
tasveer kheenchiye kisi mauj-e-khayal ki
'nasir' bahut si khawahishen dil men hai beqarar
lekin kahan se laaoon vo befikr zindagi (12)

गलियों में अब तो शाम से फिरते हैं पहेदार
है कोई-कोई शम्अ सो वो भी बुझी-बुझी
ऐ रोशनी-ए-दीदा-ओ-दिल अब नज़र भी आ
दुनिया तेरे फ़िराक़ में अंधेर हो गयी (8)
अलक़िस्सा जेब चाक ही करनी पड़ी हमें
गो इब्तिदा-ए-ग़म में बड़ी एहतियात की
अब जी में है कि सर किसी पत्थर से फोड़िये
मुमकिन है क़ल्ब-ए-संग से निकले कोई परी
बेकार बैठे रहने से बेहतर है कोई दिन
तस्वीर खींचिए किसी मौज-ए-ख़याल की
'नासिर' बहुत सी ख़्वाहिशें दिल में है बेक़रार
लेकिन कहाँ से लाऊँ वो बेफ़िक्र ज़िन्दगी (12)

4. Friends, loyalty now has for us new scripts

Guards now patrol the streets from evening
The Lights glow dim, few and far between

Oh, light of eyes and heart, show your spark
In your absence the world has turned dark (8)

To cut it short, I ended up in tatters* ultimately
Though I took caution in early phases of misery

I feel like breaking my head on a stone now
Quite possible, from its heart a fairy may glow

Instead of sitting idle for days, it'd be better
If I draw the flight of my fancy in a picture

'Nasir', my heart is aflush with many a desire
But how can I have a life of no worry, no care (12)

*Reference to the story of Majnu

5. *apni dhun men rahta hun*

apni dhun men rahta hun
main bhi tere jaisa hun
o pichhli rut ke sathi
ab ke baras main tanha hun
teri gali men saara din
dukh ke kankar chunata hun
mujh se aankh milaye kaun
main tera aina hun (4)
mera diya jalaye kaun
main tera khali kamra hun
tere siva mujhe pahne kaun
main tere tan ka kapda hun
tu jeevan ki bhari gali
main jangal ka rasta hun
aati rut mujhe royegi
jaati rut ka jhonka hun (8)
apni lahr hai apna rog
dariya hun aur pyasa hun

अपनी धुन में रहता हूँ
मैं भी तेरे जैसा हूँ
ओ पिछली रुत के साथी
अब के बरस मैं तन्हा हूँ
तेरी गली में सारा दिन
दुख के कंकर चुनता हूँ
मुझ से आँख मिलाए कौन
मैं तेरा आईना हूँ (4)
मेरा दिया जलाए कौन
मैं तिरा ख़ाली कमरा हूँ
तेरे सिवा मुझे पहने कौन
मैं तिरे तन का कपड़ा हूँ
तू जीवन की भरी गली
मैं जंगल का रस्ता हूँ
आती रुत मुझे रोएगी
जाती रुत का झोंका हूँ (8)
अपनी लहर है अपना रोग
दरिया हूँ और प्यासा हूँ

5. I stay lost in myself

I stay lost in myself
Just the way you do

Mate of my last season,
I am alone this time too

I keep going up your street
Gathering the debris of my woe

Who will look into my eyes
They reflect an image of you (4)

Who will light me up
A vacant room I am for you

Who, except you, will put on
The dress that I am for you

You are life's bustling street
I am trail in a jungle blue

Next season will mourn me
It is my last before I bid adieu (8)

My whims are my sickness
I am the river and thirsty too

6. *araaish-e-khayal bhi ho dil-kusha bhi ho*

araaish-e-khayal bhi ho dil-kusha bhi ho
vo dard ab kahan jise ji chahta bhi ho
ye kya ki roz ek sa gham ek si umeed
is ranj-e-bekhumar ki ab intiha bhi ho
ye kya ki ek taur se guzre tamaam umr
ji chahta hai ab koyi tere siva bhi ho
Tute kabhi to khwab-e-shab-o-roz ka tilism
itne hujoom men koi chehra naya bhi ho (4)
deewangi-e-shauq ko ye dhun hai in dinon
ghar bhi ho aur bedar-o-deewar sa bhi ho
juz dil koyi makaan nahin dahr men jahan
rahzan ka khauf bhi na rahe dar khula bhi ho

आराइश-ए-ख़याल भी हो दिल-कुशा भी हो
वो दर्द अब कहाँ जिसे जी चाहता भी हो
ये क्या कि रोज़ एक सा ग़म एक सी उमीद
इस रंज-ए-बे-ख़ुमार की अब इंतिहा भी हो
ये क्या कि एक तौर से गुज़रे तमाम उम्र
जी चाहता है अब कोई तेरे सिवा भी हो
टूटे कभी तो ख़्वाब-ए-शब-ओ-रोज़ का तिलिस्म
इतने हुजूम में कोई चेहरा नया भी हो (4)
दीवानगी-ए-शौक़ को ये धुन है इन दिनों
घर भी हो और बे-दर-ओ-दीवार सा भी हो
जुज़ दिल कोई मकान नहीं दहर में जहाँ
रहज़न का ख़ौफ़ भी न रहे दर खुला भी हो

--continue--

6. A thought ought to be beautiful and moving too

A thought ought to be beautiful and moving too
But where is the pain now that heart craves too

It is the same sorrow and same hope everyday
Can I have an end to this unexciting run, if I may

What monotony to have the same thing each day
Wish there were someone other than you, I pray

Will someone break the spell of everyday musing
Can there be a new face in the vast crowding (4)

Of late, a crazy longing has possessed me anew
I should be without walls and house-bound too

There is no house in the world except heart where
Robbers can cause no harm even if it is laid bare
--continue--

6. araaish-e-khayal bhi ho dil-kusha bhi ho

har zarra ek mahmil-e-ibrat hai dasht ka
lekin kise dikhaun koi dekhta bhi ho
har shai pukarti hai pas-e-parda-e-sukoot
lekin kise sunaun koi hamnava bhi ho (8)
fursat men sun shaguftagi-e-ghunche ki sadaa
ye vo sukhan nahin jo kisi ne kaha bhi ho
baitha hai ek shakhs mere paas der se
koyi bhala sa ho to hamen dekhta bhi ho
bazm-e-sukhan bhi ho sukhan-e-garm ke liye
taus bolta ho to jangal hara bhi ho

हर ज़र्रा एक महमिल-ए-इबरत है दश्त का
लेकिन किसे दिखाऊँ कोई देखता भी हो
हर शय पुकारती है पस-ए-पर्दा-ए-सुकूत
लेकिन किसे सुनाऊँ कोई हम-नवा भी हो (8)
फुर्सत में सुन शगुफ़्तगी-ए-गुंचे की सदा
ये वो सुखन नहीं जो किसी ने कहा भी हो
बैठा है एक शख़्स मिरे पास देर से
कोई भला सा हो तो हमें देखता भी हो
बज़्म-ए-सुख़न भी हो सुख़न-ए-गर्म के लिए
ताऊस बोलता हो तो जंगल हरा भी हो

6. A thought ought to be beautiful and moving too

Every particle is a carrier of the desert's desolation
But who may be interested in such an observation

There are voices calling behind the veil of stillness
But who can I tell unless they shares my likeness (8)

Listen at leisure the ditties that blooming buds sing
These are not words that anybody can ever think

For long an individual has been sitting by my side
If someone has the insight, he can have us spied

Intense poetry demands equally involved audience
Peacocks sing only when there is green ambience

7. *avvalin chand ne kya baat sujhaayi mujh ko*

avvalin chand ne kya baat sujhaayi mujh ko
yaad aayi teri angusht-e-hinaayi mujh ko
sar-e-aivan-e-tarab naghma-sara tha koyi
raat bhar us ne teri yaad dilaayi mujh ko
dekhte dekhte taron ka safar khatm hua
so gaya chand magar neend na aayi mujh ko
inhi ankhon ne dikhaye kayi bharpur jamal
inhi ankhon ne shab-e-hijr dikhaayi mujh ko (4)
saaye ki tarah mere saath rahe ranj-o-alam
gardish-e-waqt kahin raas na aayi mujh ko
dhup idhar dhalti thi dil doobta jaata tha idhar
aaj tak yaad hai vo shaam-e-judaayi mujh ko
shahr-e-Lahore teri raunaqen daaim abaad
teri galiyon ki hava kheench ke laayi mujh ko

अव्वलीं चाँद ने क्या बात सुझाई मुझ को
याद आई तिरी अंगुश्त-ए-हिनाई मुझ को
सर-ए-ऐवान-ए-तरब नग़मा-सरा था कोई
रात भर उस ने तिरी याद दिलाई मुझ को
देखते देखते तारों का सफ़र ख़त्म हुआ
सो गया चाँद मगर नींद न आई मुझ को
इन्ही आँखों ने दिखाए कई भरपूर जमाल
इन्हीं आँखों ने शब-ए-हिज्र दिखाई मुझ को (4)
साए की तरह मिरे साथ रहे रंज ओ अलम
गर्दिश-ए-वक़्त कहीं रास न आई मुझ को
धूप इधर ढलती थी दिल डूबता जाता था इधर
आज तक याद है वो शाम-ए-जुदाई मुझ को
शहर-ए-लाहौर तिरी रौनक़ें दाइम आबाद
तेरी गलियों की हवा खींच के लाई मुझ को

7. The sight of the new moon is a dead ringer

The sight of the new moon is a dead ringer
Reminds me of your henna-dyed finger

Someone crooning at a house of delight
Reminded me of you the whole night

As I watched on, stars ended their journey
The moon too went to sleep, but not me

These eyes offered me many a high marvel
The night of separation was its gift as well (4)

Worries and woes followed me like a shadow
The cycle of time did I never learn to follow

With the Sun, my heart went down too
Can't forget the eve I parted from you

May Lahore, its splendor prosper forever
The ambience of its streets pulled me here

8. bane-banaye hue raaston pe ja nikle

Bane banaye hue raston pe jaa nikle
ye hamsafar mere kitne gurez-paa nikle
chale the aur kisi raaste ki dhun men magar
ham ittefaq se teri gali men aa nikle
gham-e-firaq men kuchh der ro hi lene do
bukhaar kuchh to dil-e-beqaraar kaa nikle
nasihaten hamen karte hain tark-e-ulfat ki
ye khair-khwah hamare kidhar se aa nikle (4)
ye khamoshi to rag-o-pai men rach gayi 'nasir'
vo naala kar ki dil-e-sang se sadaa nikle

बने-बनाए हुए रास्तों पे जा निकले
ये हमसफ़र मिरे कितने गुरेज़-पा निकले
चले थे और किसी रास्ते की धुन में मगर
हम इत्तिफ़ाक़ से तेरी गली में आ निकले
ग़म-ए-फ़िराक़ में कुछ देर रो ही लेने दो
बुख़ार कुछ तो दिल-ए-बेक़रार का निकले
नसीहतें हमें करते हैं तर्क-ए-उल्फ़त की
ये ख़ैर-ख़्वाह हमारे किधर से आ निकले (4)
ये ख़ामुशी तो रग-ओ-पै में रच गई 'नासिर'
वो नाला कर कि दिल-ए-संग से सदा निकले

8. They took the path that was much travelled

They took the path that was much travelled
My friends turned out to be wary and laggard

We set off with an intent to trek a new terrain
But with luck and chance ended up in your lane

Let me cry in this hour of sorrow and separation
Hope it subsides the temper of heart's agitation

They tell us to keep away from love and desire
Who are these well-wishers and from where (4)

This silence has settled deep in your gut 'Nasir'
Bewail so loud that even a stone heart will stir

9. *basa huya hai khayalon men koyi paikar-e-naaz*

basa huya hai khayalon men koyi paikar-e-naaz
bula rahi hai abhi tak vo dilnashin awaaz
vahi dinon men tapish hai vahi shabon men gudaaz
magar ye kya ki meri zindagi men soz na saaz
na chhed ai khalish-e-dard baar-baar na chhed
chhupaye baitha hoon seene men ek umr ke raaz
bas ab to ek hi dhun hai ki neend aa jaaye
vo din kahan ki uthayen shab-e-firaq ke naaz (4)
guzar hi jaayegi ai dost tere hijr ki raat
ki tujhse badh ke tera dard hai mera damsaaz
ye aur baat ki duniyaa na sun saki varna
sukoot-e-ahl-e-nazar hai baja-e-khud awaaz

बसा हुआ है ख़यालों में कोई पैकर-ए-नाज़
बुला रही है अभी तक वो दिलनशीं आवाज़
वही दिनों में तपिश है वही शबों में गुदाज़
मगर ये क्या कि मेरी ज़िन्दगी में सोज़ न साज़
न छेड़ ऐ ख़लिश-ए-दर्द बार-बार न छेड़
छुपाये बैठा हूँ सीने में एक उम्र के राज़
बस अब तो एक ही धुन है कि नींद आ जाए
वो दिन कहाँ कि उठाएँ शब-ए-फ़िराक़ के नाज़ (4)
गुज़र ही जाएगी ऐ दोस्त तेरे हिज्र की रात
कि तुझसे बढ़ के तिरा दर्द है मिरा दमसाज़
ये और बात कि दुनिया न सुन सकी वरना
सुकूत-ए-अह्ल-ए-नज़र है बजाए-खुद आवाज़

--continue--

9. Someone of a gentle bearing occupies my mind

Someone of a gentle bearing occupies my mind
That impelling voice keeps calling me from behind

Days have same warmth, nights the same vigour
But in my life there is neither grief nor pleasure

O nagging pain, don't try too much my patience
Buried in my heart are old secrets of conscience

'I want sleep' is now my one and only petition
Gone are days I cherished nights of separation (4)

Mate, this night without you will soon be over
As more than you, this pain is now my partner

It is another matter the world did not listen to it
But the silence of the far-sighted had a voice in it
$\qquad$ --continue—

9. basa huya hai khayalon men koyi paikar-e-naaz

ye besabab naheen shaam-o-sahar ke hangamen
utha raha hai koyi parda-ha-e-raaz-o-niyaaz
tera khayal bhi teri tarah mukammal hai
vahi shabab vahi dilkashi vahi andaaz (8)
sharab-o-sher ki duniya badal gayi lekin
vo aankh dhoondh hi leti hai bekhudi ka javaaz
urooj par hai mera dard in dinon 'nasir'
meri gazal men dhadkati hai vaqt ki awaaz

ये बेसबब नहीं शाम-ओ-सहर के हंगामें
उठा रहा है कोई परदा-हा-ए-राज़-ओ-नियाज़
तिरा ख़याल भी तेरी तरह मुकम्मल है
वही शबाब वही दिलकशी वही अंदाज़ (8)
शराब-ओ-शे'र की दुनिया बदल गयी लेकिन
वो आँख ढूँढ ही लेती है बेख़ुदी का जवाज़
उरुज पर है मेरा दर्द इन दिनों 'नासिर'
मेरी ग़ज़ल में धड़कती है वक़्त की आवाज़

9. Someone of a gentle bearing occupies my mind

Not for nothing have we this day-night strife
Someone is raising curtain on the mystery of life

A thought of you is as wholesome as you are
The same beauty, same charm, same glamour (8)

The realms of wine and verse have changed, yet
The eye can find other ways to swing and forget

These days the anguish in me 'Nasir' is at its prime
At the heart of my ghazal beats the call of the time

10. *beganavaar unse mulaqaat ho to ho*

beganavaar unse mulaqaat ho to ho
ab door door hi se koyi baat ho to ho
mushkil hai fir milen kabhi yaarane-raftagan
taqdeer hi se ab ye karamaat ho to ho
unko to yaad aaye huye muddatein huyin
jeene ki vajah aur koyi baat ho to ho
kya jaanun kyon ulajhate hain vo baat-baat par
maqsad kuchh is se tarke-mulaqaat ho to ho (4)

बेगानावार उनसे मुलाक़ात हो तो हो
अब दूर दूर ही से कोई बात हो तो हो
मुश्किल है फिर मिलें कभी याराने-रफ्तगां
तक़दीर ही से अब ये करामात हो तो हो
उनको तो याद आये हुए मुद्दतें हुईं
जीने की वजह और कोई बात हो तो हो
क्या जानूँ क्यों उलझते हैं वो बात-बात पर
मक़सद कुछ इससे तर्के-मुलाक़ात हो तो हो (4)

10. Like strangers, I may meet her, if at all

Like strangers, I may meet her, if at all
Far from each other, we may talk, if at all

Little hope, lost friends will ever meet again
It will be but a miracle of luck, if at all

Her remembrance escaped me for years
What else then has kept me going, if at all

Why does she get cross at every little thing
The intent must be to break it off, if at all (4)

11. *chand gharaanon ne mil-jul kar*

chand gharaanon ne mil-jul kar
kitne gharon ka haq chheena hai
baahar ki mitti ke badale
ghar ka sona bech diya hai
sab ka bojh uthane vaale
tu is duniya men tanha hai
maili chaadar odhne vaale
tere paanv tale sona hai (4)
gahari neend se jaago 'nasir'
vo dekho sooraj nikala hai

चंद घरानों ने मिल-जुल कर
कितने घरों का हक़ छीना है
बाहर की मिट्टी के बदले
घर का सोना बेच दिया है
सबका बोझ उठाने वाले
तू इस दुनिया में तनहा है
मैली चादर ओढ़ने वाले
तेरे पाँव तले सोना है (4)
गहरी नींद से जागो 'नासिर'
वो देखो सूरज निकला है

11. A few families with their joint might

A few families with their joint might
Robbed many a home of their right

In the temptation of overseas dirt
We sold our family's gold bright

You who carry our entire burden
Soon shall be left alone to fight

You who cover yourself in rags
Have gold hidden under your stride (4)

Get out of your deep slumber 'Nasir'
Up above is the Sun full and bright

12. *dafatan dil men kisi yaad ne li angdaayi*

dafatan dil men kisi yaad ne li angdaayi
is kharabe men ye deewar kahan se aayi
aaj khulne hi ko tha dard-e-mohabbat ka bharam
vo to kahiye ki achanak hi teri yaad aayi
bas yun hi dil ko tavaqqo si hai tujh se varna
jaanta hun ki muqaddar hai mera tanhaayi
nashsha-e-talkhi-e-ayaam utarta hi nahin
teri nazron ne gulabi to bahut chhalkaayi (4)
yun to har shaksh akela hai bhari duniya men
phir bhi har dil ke muqaddar men nahin tanhaayi
yun to milne ko vo har roz hi milta hai magar
dekh kar aaj use aankh bahut lalchaayi
doobte chand pe royi hain hazaaron ankhen
main to roya bhi nahin tum ko hansi kyun aayi
raat bhar jagte rahte ho bhala kyun 'nasir'
tum ne ye daulat-e-bedar kahan se paayi (8)

दफ़अतन दिल में किसी याद ने ली अँगड़ाई
इस ख़राबे में ये दीवार कहाँ से आई
आज खुलने को ही था दर्द-ए-मुहब्बत का भरम
वो तो कहिए कि अचानक ही तेरी याद आई
बस यूँ ही दिल को तवक़्क़ो सी है तुझ से वर्ना
जानता हूँ कि मुक़द्दर है मिरा तन्हाई
नश्शा-ए-तलख़ी-ए-अय्याम उतरता ही नहीं
तेरी नज़रों ने गुलाबी तो बहुत छलकाई (4)
यूँ तो हर शख़्स अकेला है भरी दुनिया में
फिर भी हर दिल के मुक़द्दर में नहीं तन्हाई
यूँ तो मिलने को वो हर रोज़ ही मिलता है मगर
देखकर आज उसे आँख बहुत ललचाई
डूबते चाँद पर रोई हैं हज़ारों आँखें
मैं तो रोया भी नहीं तुमको हँसी क्यों आई
रात भर जागते रहते हो भला क्यों 'नासिर'
तुमने ये दौलत-ए-बेदार कहाँ से पाई (8)

12. In my heart a memory suddenly took a turn

In my heart a memory suddenly took a turn
How did a wall come up in this wretched ruin

The myth about love-ache was about to go
When suddently your memory came up too

In my heart, hope from you has a little spot
Though I know loneliness is all but my lot

The hangover of daily woes does not shrink
Even when your eyes offer me a pink drink (4)

Though everyone in the world is on his own
Yet every heart is not destined to be alone

As a matter of routine, we meet every day
Desire in particular tempted my eyes today

When the moon sets in a thousand eyes cry
Why did you giggle when I didn't even sigh

Why do you 'Nasir', spend nights sleepless
Where did you receive this bounty of unrest (8)

13. *dayar-e-dil ki raat men charagh sa jala gaya*

dayar-e-dil ki raat men charagh sa jala gaya
mila nahin to kya hua vo shakl to dikha gaya
vo dosti to khair ab nasib-e-dushmana huyi
vo chhoti chhoti ranjishon ka lutf bhi chala gaya
judaaiyon ke zakhm dard-e-zindagi ne bhar diye
tujhe bhi neend aa gayi mujhe bhi sabr aa gaya
pukarti hain fursaten kahan gayin vo sohbaten
zamin nigal gai unhen ki aasman kha gaya (4)
ye subah ki safediyan ye dopahar ki zardiyan
ab aaine men dekhta hun main kahan chala gaya
ye kis khushi ki ret par ghamon ko neend aa gayi
vo lahr kis taraf gayi main kahan sama gaya
gaye dinon ki laash par pade rahoge kab talak
alam-kasho utho ki aaftab sar pe aa gaya

दयार-ए-दिल की रात में चराग़ सा जला गया
मिला नहीं तो क्या हुआ वो शक्ल तो दिखा गया
वो दोस्ती तो ख़ैर अब नसीब-ए-दुश्मनाँ हुई
वो छोटी छोटी रंजिशों का लुत्फ़ भी चला गया
जुदाइयों के ज़ख़्म दर्द-ए-ज़िंदगी ने भर दिए
तुझे भी नींद आ गई मुझे भी सब्र आ गया
पुकारती हैं फ़ुर्सतें कहाँ गईं वो सोहबतें
ज़मीं निगल गई उन्हें कि आसमान खा गया (4)
ये सुब्ह की सफ़ेदियाँ ये दोपहर की ज़र्दियाँ
अब आइने में देखता हूँ मैं कहाँ चला गया
ये किस ख़ुशी की रेत पर ग़मों को नींद आ गई
वो लहर किस तरफ़ गई ये मैं कहाँ समा गया
गए दिनों की लाश पर पड़े रहोगे कब तलक
अलम-कशो उठो कि आफ़्ताब सर पे आ गया

13. Someone lit a candle in the dark corner of my heart

Someone lit a candle in the dark corner of my heart
With his brief appearance, but left soon to depart

Amity turning into hostility left one thing wanting
It took away the tender delight of small nagging

The sores of split were healed by other pains of life
You found a good sleep, I found solace in being safe

When in leisure, I hear voices of bonhomie we had
Did the earth swallow them or heavens went mad? (4)

Looking at the grey in the morning and pale in noon
I ask the mirror where have I moved to, so soon

In which happy shores have sorrows taken a rest
Where has this tide turned and left me submersed

How long will you bewail over days gone dead
Mourners! Wake up, the sun is blazing overhead

14. *dekh mohabbat ka dastoor*

dekh mohabbat ka dastoor
tu mujh se main tujh se door
tanha tanha phirte hain
dil viran ankhen benoor
dost bichhadte jaate hain
shauq liye jaata hai door
ham apna gham bhul gaye
aaj kise dekha majboor (4)
dil ki dhadkan kahti hai
aaj koi aayega zaroor
koshish laazim hai pyare
aage jo us ko manzoor
suraj doob chala 'nasir'
aur abhi manzil hai door

देख मोहब्बत का दस्तूर
तू मुझ से मैं तुझ से दूर
तन्हा तन्हा फिरते हैं
दिल वीराँ आँखें बे-नूर
दोस्त बिछड़ते जाते हैं
शौक़ लिए जाता है दूर
हम अपना ग़म भूल गए
आज किसे देखा मजबूर (4)
दिल की धड़कन कहती है
आज कोई आएगा ज़रूर
कोशिश लाज़िम है प्यारे
आगे जो उस को मंज़ूर
सूरज डूब चला 'नासिर'
और अभी मंज़िल है दूर

14. Look at love and its way

Look at love and its way
I'm here and you far away

We split our ways to go alone
With hearts heavy, eyes to mourn

Friends are parting one by one
Far have we moved in passion

I forgot all about my sorrows
When I saw one in deeper woes (4)

The heartbeat augurs good today
Someone I love must be on the way

We can't stop making efforts
Though He decides what one gets

'Nasir' the Sun is going to descend
But far still is the journey's end

15. *dil dhadakne ka sabab yaad aaya*

dil dhadakne ka sabab yaad aaya
vo teri yaad thi ab yaad aaya
aaj mushkil tha sambhalna ai dost
tu musibat men ajab yaad aaya
din guzara tha badi mushkil se
phir tera vaada-e-shab yaad aaya
tera bhula hua paiman-e-vafa
mar rahenge agar ab yaad aaya (4)
phir kayi log nazar se guzre
phir koi shahr-e-tarab yaad aaya
haal-e-dil ham bhi sunaate lekin
jab vo rukhsat huya tab yaad aaya
baith kar saaya-e-gul men 'nasir'
ham bahut roye vo jab yaad aaya

दिल धड़कने का सबब याद आया
वो तिरी याद थी अब याद आया
आज मुश्किल था सँभलना ऐ दोस्त
तू मुसीबत में अजब याद आया
दिन गुज़ारा था बड़ी मुश्किल से
फिर तिरा वादा-ए-शब याद आया
तेरा भूला हुआ पैमान-ए-वफ़ा
मर रहेंगे अगर अब याद आया (4)
फिर कई लोग नज़र से गुज़रे
फिर कोई शहर-ए-तरब याद आया
हाल-ए-दिल हम भी सुनाते लेकिन
जब वो रुख़्सत हुआ तब याद आया
बैठ कर साया-ए-गुल में 'नासिर'
हम बहुत रोए वो जब याद आया

15. Why the heart missed a beat, I know

Why the heart missed a beat, I know
A thought of you gave a knock, I know

Today I found myself tough to control
In tough times, how I miss you, I know

The day was hard to endure, but then
Your promise for the night, I know

Your unto-the-last pledge that I forgot
If revived now, will kill me, I know (4)

Hordes of people filed past the eye
Reminded me of a city of joy, I know

I could have shared my heart with her
It came to mind after she left, I know

Sitting under a blooming bower, 'Nasir'
I cried a lot when I missed her, I know

16. *dil men aur to kya rakha hai*

dil men aur to kya rakha hai
tera dard chhupa rakha hai
itne dukhon ki tez hawa men
dil ka deep jala rakha hai
dhup se chehron ne duniya men
kya andher macha rakha hai
is nagri ke kuchh logon ne
dukh ka naam dawa rakha hai (4)
vaada-e-yaar ki baat na chhedo
ye dhoka bhi kha rakha hai
bhool bhi jaayo beeti baaten
in baaton men kya rakha hai
chup chup kyun rahte ho 'nasir'
ye kya rog laga rakha hai

दिल में और तो क्या रक्खा है
तेरा दर्द छुपा रक्खा है
इतने दुखों की तेज़ हवा में
दिल का दीप जला रक्खा है
धूप से चेहरों ने दुनिया में
क्या अंधेर मचा रक्खा है
इस नगरी के कुछ लोगों ने
दुख का नाम दवा रक्खा है (4)
वादा-ए-यार की बात न छेड़ो
ये धोका भी खा रक्खा है
भूल भी जाओ बीती बातें
इन बातों में क्या रक्खा है
चुप चुप क्यूँ रहते हो 'नासिर'
ये क्या रोग लगा रक्खा है

16. In heart, what else can be new

In heart, what else can be new
Buried there is heartache for you

In the strong winds of despair
I keep the heart glowing too

What a dark storm sunny faces
Of the world have set up to brew

Some people in this town call
Pain a cure for misery too (4)

Don't talk about the lover's oath
For me this trickery is not new

Let us forget what happened
Why talk, there's nothing new

Why stay ever tight-lipped, Nasir
What is this malaise with you

17. *dil men ik lehar si uthi hai abhi*

dil men ik lehar si uthi hai abhi
koyi taaza hava chali hai abhi
kuchh to nazuk mizaj hain ham bhi
aur ye chot bhi nayi hai abhi
shor barpa hai khaana-e-dil men
koyi deewar si giri hai abhi
bhari duniya men ji nahin lagta
jaane kis cheez ki kami hai abhi (4)
tu sharik-e-sukhan nahin hai to kya
ham-sukhan teri khamoshi hai abhi
yaad ke be-nishan jaziron se
teri awaaz aa rahi hai abhi

दिल में इक लहर सी उठी है अभी
कोई ताज़ा हवा चली है अभी
कुछ तो नाज़ुक मिज़ाज हैं हम भी
और ये चोट भी नई है अभी
शोर बरपा है ख़ाना-ए-दिल में
कोई दीवार सी गिरी है अभी
भरी दुनिया में जी नहीं लगता
जाने किस चीज़ की कमी है अभी (4)
तू शरीक-ए-सुख़न नहीं है तो क्या
हम-सुख़न तेरी ख़ामुशी है अभी
याद के बे-निशाँ जज़ीरों से
तेरी आवाज़ आ रही है अभी

--continue--

17. Something like a tide surged in me now

Something like a tide surged in me now
A fresh air breezed past me perhaps just now

Though somewhat naïve and delicate I am
This hurt is fresh and tender too right now

A rumble came up in the corner of my heart
It seems a wall came down tumbling just now

I don't feel at home in this teeming world
I don't know what I want, what I miss now (4)

What if you are not much in conversation
Your silence is as much a partner right now

In the unmarked islands of our lost memories
Your far away voice reverberates even now
        --continue--

17. dil men ik lehar si uthi hai abhi

shahar ki be-charagh galiyon men
zindagi tujh ko dhundti hai abhi
so gaye log us haveli ke
ek khidki magar khuli hai abhi (8)
tum to yaaro abhi se uth baithe
shehar men raat jaagti hai abhi
waqt achha bhi aayega 'nasir'
gham na kar zindagi padi hai abhi

शहर की बे-चराग़ गलियों में
ज़िंदगी तुझ को ढूँडती है अभी
सो गए लोग उस हवेली के
एक खिड़की मगर खुली है अभी (8)
तुम तो यारो अभी से उठ बैठे
शहर में रात जागती है अभी
वक़्त अच्छा भी आएगा 'नासिर'
ग़म न कर ज़िंदगी पड़ी है अभी

17. Something like a tide surged in me now

In the unlit alleys of this heartbreak town
My heart and soul look for you even now

Everybody has gone to sleep in that big house
A casement, though, remains open even now(8)

Friends, you have wrapped up the gathering
But the night is young, the city alive even now

Time will turn, we will have good times 'Nasir'
Don't you worry, there is still life ahead of now

18. *dukh ki lehar ne chheda hoga*

dukh ki lehar ne chheda hoga
yaad ne kankar phenka hoga
aaj to mera dil kahta hai
tu is waqt akela hoga
mere chume huye hathon se
auron ko khat likhta hoga
bheeg chalin ab raat ki palken
tu ab thak kar soya hoga (4)
rail ki gahri seeti sun kar
raat ka jangal gunja hoga
shehar ke khali station par
koi musafir utra hoga
angan men phir chidiyan bolin
tu ab so kar uttha hoga
yadon ki jalti shabnam se
phool sa mukhda dhoya hoga (8)

दुख की लहर ने छेड़ा होगा
याद ने कंकर फेंका होगा
आज तो मेरा दिल कहता है
तू इस वक़्त अकेला होगा
मेरे चूमे हुए हाथों से
औरों को ख़त लिखता होगा
भीग चलीं अब रात की पलकें
तू अब थक कर सोया होगा (4)
रेल की गहरी सीटी सुन कर
रात का जंगल गूँजा होगा
शहर के ख़ाली स्टेशन पर
कोई मुसाफ़िर उतरा होगा
आँगन में फिर चिड़ियाँ बोलीं
तू अब सो कर उट्ठा होगा
यादों की जलती शबनम से
फूल सा मुखड़ा धोया होगा (8)

--continue--

18. A swirl of pain may have started it

A swirl of pain may have started it
Memory may have shot a stone in it

Today I have this feeling in my bone
At this time, you may be all alone

The hands that I once kissed as ours
May now be writing letters to others

Nightly Eyelids now must be wet
Tired, you may have retired to bed (4)

At night, sonorous whistle of a train
May have echoed in the jungle terrain

On a deserted bay of a railway town
A lonely traveller may have got down

Birds started tweeting in the street
You may have now stirred out of sleep

With memory's seething dewy haze
You may have washed your flower face (8)
--continue--

18. dukh ki lehar ne chheda hoga

moti jaisi shakl bana kar
aaine ko takta hoga
shaam hui ab tu bhi shayad
apne ghar ko lauta hoga
neeli dhundli khamoshi men
taron ki dhun sunta hoga
mera sathi shaam ka taara
tujh se aankh milata hoga (12)
shaam ke chalte haath ne tujh ko
mera salam to bheja hoga
pyasi kurlaati kunjon ne
mera dukh to sunaaya hoga
main to aaj bahut roya hun
tu bhi shayad roya hoga
'nasir' tera meet puraana
tujh ko yaad to aata hoga (16)

मोती जैसी शक्ल बना कर
आईने को तकता होगा
शाम हुई अब तू भी शायद
अपने घर को लौटा होगा
नीली धुंदली ख़ामोशी में
तारों की धुन सुनता होगा
मेरा साथी शाम का तारा
तुझ से आँख मिलाता होगा (12)
शाम के चलते हाथ ने तुझ को
मेरा सलाम तो भेजा होगा
प्यासी कुर्लाती कूंजों ने
मेरा दुख तो सुनाया होगा
मैं तो आज बहुत रोया हूँ
तू भी शायद रोया होगा
'नासिर' तेरा मीत पुराना
तुझ को याद तो आता होगा (16)

18. A swirl of pain may have started it

With face poised like a pearl jewel
You may be looking the mirror in full

It is evening time, and probably you
Have returned to your home too

In the blue silence of a night vaporous
You may be listening to the stars' chorus

My companion, the evening star
May be eyeing you from that far (12)

By evening, a hand salute of mine
Must have reached you in time

The honking, wailing thirsty geese
May have conveyed you my miseries

I spent the day today crying a lot
You too may have, perhaps, I thought

'Nasir' is your friend from old times
Do you miss him too sometimes (16)

19. *fikr-e-taamir-e-aashiyan bhi hai*

*fikr-e-taamir-e-aashiyan bhi hai
Khauf-e-bemehri-e-khizan bhi hai
khaak bhi ud rahi hai raston men
aamad-e-subah ka saman bhi hai
rang bhi ud raha hai phoolon ka
ghunche ghunche sharar-fishan bhi hai
os bhi hai kahin kahin larzan
bazm-e-anjum dhuan dhuan bhi hai (4)
kuchh to mausam bhi hai khayal-angez
kuchh tabiyat meri ravan bhi hai
kuchh tera husn bhi hai hosh-ruba
kuchh meri shokhi-e-bayan bhi hai
har nafas shauq bhi hai manzil ka
har qadam yaad-e-raftagan bhi hai
vajeh-e-taskeen bhi hai khayal us ka
had se badh jaaye to giran bhi hai (8)
zindagi jis ke dam se hai 'nasir'
yaad us ki azaab-e-jaan bhi hai*

फ़िक्र-ए-तामीर-ए-आशियाँ भी है
ख़ौफ़-ए-बेमेहरी-ए-ख़िज़ाँ भी है
ख़ाक भी उड़ रही है रस्तों में
आमद-ए-सुब्ह का समाँ भी है
रंग भी उड़ रहा है फूलों का
गुंचे गुंचे शरर-फ़िशाँ भी है
ओस भी है कहीं कहीं लर्ज़ाँ
बज़्म-ए-अंजुम धुआँ धुआँ भी है (4)
कुछ तो मौसम भी है ख़याल-अंगेज़
कुछ तबीअत मिरी रवाँ भी है
कुछ तिरा हुस्न भी है होश-रुबा
कुछ मिरी शोख़ी-ए-बयाँ भी है
हर नफ़स शौक़ भी है मंज़िल का
हर क़दम याद-ए-रफ़्तगाँ भी है
वजह-ए-तस्कीं भी है ख़याल उस का
हद से बढ़ जाए तो गिराँ भी है (8)
ज़िंदगी जिस के दम से है 'नासिर'
याद उस की अज़ाब-ए-जाँ भी है

19. If I have worries about making a nest

If I have worries about making a nest
A fear lurks about the cruel autumn too

There are clouds of dirt in the streets
Yet it is time for a new morning too

I can see colours fading out of flowers
Yet new buds have a spark of fire too

Though dew hangs in some corners
Yet haze is shadowing the stars too (4)

This season is no doubt spiking ideas
I find myself in some active mood too

Your beauty is indeed mind blowing
But there is a flourish in my telling too

Every breath is a step towards the goal
Yet it is a reminder of the past too

A thought of hers gives me some peace
But if it gets too much, it is a burden too (8)

A remembrance that sustains my life
Brings for 'Nasir' a huge suffering too

20. *gaa raha tha koyi darakhaton men*

gaa raha tha koyi darakhaton men
raat neend aa gayi darakhaton men
chaand nikala ufaq ke gaaron se
aag si lag gayi darakhaton men
mehn jo barsa to bargrezon ne
chhed di baansuri darakhaton men
ye hava thi ki dhyaan ka jhonka
kis ne awaaz di darakhaton men (4)
ham idhar ghar men ho gaye bechain
door aandhi chali darakhaton men
liye jaati hai mausamon ki pukar
ajanabi-ajanabi darakhaton men

गा रहा था कोई दरख़्तों में
रात नींद आ गई दरख़्तों में
चाँद निकला उफ़क़ के ग़ारों से
आग सी लग गई दरख़्तों में
मेंह जो बरसा तो बगरिज़ों ने
छेड़ दी बाँसुरी दरख़्तों में
ये हवा थी कि ध्यान का झोंका
किसने आवाज़ दी दरख़्तों में (4)
हम इधर घर में हो गये बेचैन
दूर आँधी चली दरख़्तों में
लिये जाती है मौसमों की पुकार
अजनबी-अजनबी दरख़्तों में
--continue--

20. I heard someone croon in the trees

I heard someone croon in the trees
I fell asleep last night in the trees

Rising from the depths of the horizon,
The moon fired a blaze in the trees

The dry leaves with pattering of rain
Drummed up a symphony in the trees

Was it the wind or a whisper in mind?
I heard someone call me in the trees (4)

Here in our homes we got restless
Far away a gale erupted in the trees

The call of different seasons takes
Me to a strange range in the trees
                      --continue--

20. gaa raha tha koyi darakhaton men

kitni aabadiyan hain shehr se door
jaake dekho kabhi darakhton men
neele, peele, safed, laal, hare
rang dekho sabhi darakhaton men (8)
khushbuyon ki udaas shahzaadi
raat mujh ko mili darakhaton men
der tak us ki tez aankhon se
roshani si rahi darakhaton men
chalate-chalate dagar ujaalon ki
jaane kyon mud gayi darakhaton men
sahme-sahme the raat ahl-e-chaman
tha koyi aadami darakhaton men (12)

कितनी आबादियाँ हैं शहर से दूर
जाके देखो कभी दरख़्तों में
नीले, पीले, सफेद, लाल, हरे
रंग देखो सभी दरख़्तों में (8)
ख़ुशबुओं की उदास शहज़ादी
रात मुझको मिली दरख़्तों में
देर तक उसकी तेज़ आँखों से
रोशनी सी रही दरख़्तों में
चलते-चलते डगर उजालों की
जाने क्यों मुड़ गई दरख़्तों में
सहमे-सहमे थे रात अह्ल-ए-चमन
था कोई आदमी दरख़्तों में (12)

20. I heard someone croon in the trees

There are colonies beyond the cities
Go have a close look in the trees

Blue, pale, white, red and emerald
You can have all hues in the trees (8)

The forlorn fairy of lost fragrances
Met me last night in the trees

The radiance of her eyes for long
Bestowed brilliance to the trees

Why did the lighted street in its run
Suddently turned towards the trees?

Inmates of the woods were alarmed
A man in dark was lurking in the trees (12)

21. *gali gali abaad thi jin se kahan gaye vo log*

gali gali abaad thi jin se kahan gaye vo log
dilli ab ke aisi ujadi ghar ghar phaila sog
saara saara din galiyon men phirte hain bekar
raaton uth uth kar rote hain is nagri ke log
sahme sahme se baithe hain raagi aur fankar
bhor bhaye ab in galiyon men kaun sunaye jog
jab tak ham masruf rahe ye duniya thi sunsaan
din dhalte hi dhyaan men aaye kaise kaise log (4)
'nasir' ham ko raat mila tha tanha aur udaas
vahi purani baaten us ki vahi purana rog

गली गली आबाद थी जिन से कहाँ गए वो लोग
दिल्ली अब के ऐसी उजड़ी घर घर फैला सोग
सारा सारा दिन गलियों में फिरते हैं बेकार
रातों उठ उठ कर रोते हैं इस नगरी के लोग
सहमे सहमे से बैठे हैं रागी और फ़नकार
भोर भए अब इन गलियों में कौन सुनाए जोग
जब तक हम मसरूफ़ रहे ये दुनिया थी सुनसान
दिन ढलते ही ध्यान में आए कैसे कैसे लोग (4)
'नासिर' हम को रात मिला था तन्हा और उदास
वही पुरानी बातें उस की वही पुराना रोग

21. Who kept the streets abuzz, where are they

Who kept the streets abuzz, where are they
The destruction of Delhi has left all in disarray

Daytime they idle away aimlessly in the streets
At night the people sob in half-awake sleeps

Frightened are they, the artists and musicians
Who would chant in streets the morning hymns

In the rush of the day, the mind gets blanked out
By sun down again, all those people it calls out (4)

Last night I met 'Nasir', lonesome and sombre
With the same old stories and same old temper

22. *gali gali meri yaad bichhi hai pyare rasta dekh ke chal*

*gali gali meri yaad bichhi hai pyare rasta dekh ke chal
mujh se itni vahshat hai to meri hadon se door nikal
ek samay tera phool sa nazuk haath tha mere shanon par
ek ye waqt ki main tanha aur dukh ke kanton ka jangal
ek ye waqt ki tune mujh ko dekhte hi munh pher liya
ek vo din jab tune mere paanv men rakha thaa aanchal
yaad hai ab tak tujh se bichhadne ki vo andheri shaam mujhe
tu khamosh khada tha lekin baaten karta tha kajal
main to ek nayi duniya ki dhun men bhatakta phirta hun
meri tujh se kaise nibhe gi ek hain tere fikr-o-amal (4)
mera munh kya dekh raha hai dekh is kaali raat ko dekh
main vahi tera hamrahi hun saath mere chalna ho to chal*

गली गली मिरी याद बिछी है प्यारे रस्ता देख के चल
मुझ से इतनी वहशत है तो मेरी हदों से दूर निकल
एक समय तिरा फूल सा नाजुक हाथ था मेरे शानों पर
एक ये वक़्त कि मैं तन्हा और दुख के काँटों का जंगल
एक ये वक़्त कि तूने मुझको देखते ही मुँह फेर लिया
एक वो दिन जब तूने मेरे पांव में रखा था आँचल
याद है अब तक तुझ से बिछड़ने की वो अँधेरी शाम मुझे
तू ख़ामोश खड़ा था लेकिन बातें करता था काजल (4)
मैं तो एक नई दुनिया की धुन में भटकता फिरता हूँ
मेरी तुझ से कैसे निभेगी एक हैं तेरे फ़िक्र ओ अमल
मेरा मुँह क्या देख रहा है देख इस काली रात को देख
मैं वही तेरा हमराही हूँ साथ मिरे चलना हो तो चल

22. Step cautiously, remains of me are spread all the way

Step cautiously, remains of me are spread all the way
If you have such a dread of me, stay out of my way

There was a time I had your delicate hand on my face
Today I am all alone, caught in the thickets of dismay

You turn your gaze away from me now, remember
When you spread under my feet your scarf one day

I still remember the dark evening we decided to split
You stood still, but your coal-lined eyes gave it away (4)

I fret around, losing myself in the quest of a new world
With you always at peace, can we ever together stay

Why look at me and wait, look at this pitch dark night
It is me your old pal, join me if you can, on this way

23. *gaye dinon ka suragh le kar*

*gaye dinon ka suragh le kar kidhar se aaya kidhar gaya vo
ajeeb manus ajnabi tha mujhe to hairan kar gaya vo
bas ek moti si chhab dikha kar bas ek mithi si dhun suna kar
sitara-e-sham ban ke aaya barang-e-khwab-e-sahar gaya vo
khushi ki rut ho ki gham ka mausam nazar use dhundti hai har dam
vo boo-e-gul tha ki naghma-e-jaan mere to dil men utar gaya vo
na ab vo yaadon ka chadhta dariya na fursaton ki udaas barkha
yun hi zara si kasak hai dil men jo zakhm gehra tha bhar gaya vo (4)
kuch ab sambhalne lagi hai jaan bhi badal chala daur-e-aasman bhi
jo raat bhari thi tal gayi hai jo din kada tha guzar gaya vo
bas ek manzil hai bul-havas ki hazaar raste hain ahl-e-dil ke
yahi to hai farq mujh men us men guzar gaya main thehar gaya vo*

गए दिनों का सुराग़ ले कर किधर से आया किधर गया वो
अजीब मानूस अजनबी था मुझे तो हैरान कर गया वो
बस एक मोती सी छब दिखा कर बस एक मीठी सी धुन सुना कर
सितारा-ए-शाम बन के आया ब-रंग-ए-ख़्वाब-ए-सहर गया वो
ख़ुशी की रुत हो कि ग़म का मौसम नज़र उसे ढूँडती है हर दम
वो बू-ए-गुल था कि नग़्मा-ए-जाँ मिरे तो दिल में उतर गया वो
न अब वो यादों का चढ़ता दरिया न फ़ुर्सतों की उदास बरखा
यूँही ज़रा सी कसक है दिल में जो ज़ख़्म गहरा था भर गया वो (4)
कुछ अब सँभलने लगी है जाँ भी बदल चला दौर-ए-आसमाँ भी
जो रात भारी थी टल गई है जो दिन कड़ा था गुज़र गया वो
बस एक मंज़िल है बुल-हवस की हज़ार रस्ते हैं अहल-ए-दिल के
यही तो है फ़र्क़ मुझ में उस में गुज़र गया मैं ठहर गया वो

--Continue--

23. With intimations of the past he came

With intimations of the past he came,
and went to I don't know where
Strange yet familiar he was,
but left me utterly clueless and unaware

After a flash like the glimmer of a pearl,
after playing a song dulcet
Like the evening star he appeared,
like the morning dream he vanished

Delight or pain, whatever the season,
eyes crave for him eternally
Whether scent of a flower or song of life,
deep down he sank unto me

No rising tide of old memories,
no dismal flow of vacant hours now
Just a prickly pain in the heart,
the old deep gash is repaired now (4)

Life is getting back to normal,
the sky of circumstances is getting clearer
The night of crisis has passed over,
the hard day is not cruel any longer

Obsession has only one endpoint,
loving hearts have myriad ways to go
That is the difference between us,
I moved on and he chose not to go

--Continue—

23. *gaye dinon ka suragh le kar*

shikasta-paa raah men khada hun gaye dinon ko bula raha hun
jo qafila mera hamsafar tha misaal-e-gard-e-safar gaya vo
mera to khoon ho gaya hai paani sitamgaron ki palak na bheegi
jo naala uttha tha raat dil se na jaane kyun be-asar gaya vo (8)
vo maikade ko jagaane vaala vo raat ki neend udaane vaala
ye aaj kya us ke jee men aayi ki shaam hote hi ghar gaya vo
vo hijr ki raat ka sitara vo ham-nafas ham-sukhan hamara
sada rahe us ka naam pyara suna hai kal raat mar gaya vo
vo jis ke shaane pe haath rakh kar safar kiya tune manzilon ka
teri gali se na jaane kyun aaj sar jhukaye guzar gaya vo
vo raat ka be-nava musafir vo tera shair vo tera 'nasir'
teri gali tak to ham ne dekha tha phir na jaane kidhar gaya vo (12)

शिकस्ता-पा राह में खड़ा हूँ गए दिनों को बुला रहा हूँ
जो क़ाफ़िला मेरा हम-सफ़र था मिसाल-ए-गर्द-ए-सफ़र गया वो
मिरा तो ख़ून हो गया है पानी सितमगरों की पलक न भीगी
जो नाला उट्ठा था रात दिल से न जाने क्यूँ बे-असर गया वो (8)
वो मय-कदे को जगाने वाला वो रात की नींद उड़ाने वाला
ये आज क्या उस के जी में आई कि शाम होते ही घर गया वो
वो हिज्र की रात का सितारा वो हम-नफ़स हम-सुख़न हमारा
सदा रहे उस का नाम प्यारा सुना है कल रात मर गया वो
वो जिस के शाने पे हाथ रख कर सफ़र किया तू ने मंज़िलों का
तिरी गली से न जाने क्यूँ आज सर झुकाए गुज़र गया वो
वो रात का बे-नवा मुसाफ़िर वो तेरा शाइर वो तेरा 'नासिर'
तिरी गली तक तो हम ने देखा था फिर न जाने किधर गया वो (12)

23. With intimations of the past he came

Standing midway, frustrated,
I look back and hark the days gone by
The caravan that I was part of
has dispersed too like dust on the way

The blood in me turned to water,
 the oppressor's eye remained dry
The wailing cry that rose in the night
had no effect, I don't know why (8)

The one who was life of the tavern,
who kept us awake all night
What came upon him today,
headed home before the fall of night

Star performer of the lonely nights,
a close friend, a ready raconteur
We heard he passed away last night,
may his name stay alive forever

Riding on whose shoulders,
you marched on to many a milestone
He passed by your street today,
with his head down, unbeknown

That poor penniless nightly rambler of a poet,
that yours truly 'Nasir'
Was last seen in your street,
then he vanished nobody knows where (12)

24. gham hai ya khushi hai tu

gham hai ya khushi hai tu
meri zindagi hai tu
aafaton ke daur men
chain ki ghadi hai tu
meri raat ka charagh
meri neend bhi hai tu
main khizan ki shaam hun
rut bahar ki hai tu (4)
doston ke darmiyan
vajh-e-dosti hai tu
meri saari umr men
ek hi kami hai tu
main to vo nahin raha
haan magar vahi hai tu
'nasir' is dayar men
kitna ajnabi hai tu (8)

ग़म है या ख़ुशी है तू
मेरी ज़िंदगी है तू
आफ़तों के दौर में
चैन की घड़ी है तू
मेरी रात का चराग़
मेरी नींद भी है तू
मैं ख़िज़ाँ की शाम हूँ
रुत बहार की है तू (4)
दोस्तों के दरमियाँ
वज्ह-ए-दोस्ती है तू
मेरी सारी उम्र में
एक ही कमी है तू
मैं तो वो नहीं रहा
हाँ मगर वही है तू
'नासिर' इस दयार में
कितना अजनबी है तू (8)

24. Grief or joy, what are you

Grief or joy, what are you
Though life of me are you

In times of trouble and pain
A moment of peace are you

The light in my darkness and
A good night's sleep are you

I'm eve of the autumn end
A blooming spring are you (4)

Amid camaraderie of friends
The spirit of geniality are you

What I regret most in life
Is only the absence of you

I am not my same old self
Though forever same are you

In this wilderness, 'Nasir'
How like a stranger are you (8)

25. *girafta-dil hain bahut aaj tere deewane*

girafta-dil hain bahut aaj tere deewane
khuda kare koyi tere siva na pahchane
miti miti si umeeden thake thake se khayal
bujhe bujhe se nigahon men gham ke afsane
hazaar shukr ki ham ne zaban se kuchh na kaha
ye aur baat ki puchha na ahl-e-duniya ne
ba-qadr-e-trishna-labi pursish-e-vafa na huyi
chhalak ke rah gaye teri nazar ke paimane (4)
khayal aa gaya manus rahguzaaron ka
palat ke aa gaye manzil se tere deewane
kahan hai tu ki tere intizar men ai dost
tamaam raat sulagte hain dil ke virane
umeed-e-pursish-e-gham kis se kijiye 'nasir'
jo apne dil pe guzarti hai koi kya jaane

गिरफ़्ता-दिल हैं बहुत आज तेरे दीवाने
ख़ुदा करे कोई तेरे सिवा न पहचाने
मिटी मिटी सी उमीदें थके थके से ख़याल
बुझे बुझे से निगाहों में ग़म के अफ़साने
हज़ार शुक्र कि हम ने ज़बाँ से कुछ न कहा
ये और बात कि पूछा न अहल-ए-दुनिया ने
ब-क़द्र-ए-तिश्ना-लबी पुर्सिश-ए-वफ़ा न हुई
छलक के रह गए तेरी नज़र के पैमाने (4)
ख़याल आ गया मानूस रहगुज़ारों का
पलट के आ गए मंज़िल से तेरे दीवाने
कहाँ है तू कि तिरे इंतिज़ार में ऐ दोस्त
तमाम रात सुलगते हैं दिल के वीराने
उमीद-ए-पुर्सिश-ए-ग़म किस से कीजिए 'नासिर'
जो अपने दिल पे गुज़रती है कोई क्या जाने

25. Your crazy lovers are now captives of their heart

Your crazy lovers are now captives of their heart
God forbid, none other but you see their fault

With hope fading away and muse running out
The eyes tell sorry tales that are half burnt out

Thank god, I didn't have to speak a single word
But then nobody really cared or even enquired

Like wine-craving lips, mine couldn't solicit loyalty
Tho' cheery cups of your eyes overran in plenty (4)

When they sensed the comfort of a familiar route
Your crazy lovers abandoned midway their pursuit

I Looked for you all night, where are you, mate
The arid corners of my heart burn bright in wait

Why expect someone to stand by you in grief
Who cares 'Nasir' what happens to you, in brief

26. ham jis ped ki chhaanv men baitha karate the

ham jis ped ki chhaanv men baitha karate the
ab us ped ke patte jhadte jaate hain
ek anokhee basti dhyaan men basati hai
us basti ke baasi mujhe bulaate hain
main to aankhen band kiye baitha hoon magar
dil ke darwaaze kyon khulate jaate hain
tu aankhon se ojhal hota jaata hai
door khade ham khaali haath hilaate hain (4)
jab bhee naye safar par jaata hoon 'nasir'
pichhale safar ke saathi dhyaan men aate hain.

हम जिस पेड़ की छांव में बैठा करते थे
अब उस पेड़ के पत्ते झड़ते जाते हैं
एक अनोखी बस्ती ध्यान में बसती है
उस बस्ती के बासी मुझे बुलाते हैं
मैं तो आंखें बन्द किये बैठा हूँ मगर
दिल के दरवाज़े क्यों खुलते जाते हैं
तू आंखों से ओझल होता जाता है
दूर खड़े हम खाली हाथ हिलाते हैं (4)
जब भी नये सफ़र पर जाता हूँ 'नासिर'
पिछले सफ़र के साथी ध्यान में आते हैं।

26. The shade tree we use to sit under

The shade tree we use to sit under
Is now shedding its leaves all over

A strange community lives in my head
Its inhabitants keep calling me over

I am sitting with my eyes shut, but
The doors of heart are opening as ever

You are vanishing far in the distance
From here we wave hands in vacant air (4)

Whenever I set out on a new journey
I miss the old mates of my yesteryear

27. haasil-e-ishq tera husn-e-pasheman hi sahi

haasil-e-ishq tera husn-e-pasheman hi sahi
meri hasrat teri surat se numayan hi sahi
husn bhi husn hai mohtaj-e-nazar hai jab tak
shola-e-ishq charagh-e-tah-e-daaman hi sahi
kya khabar khaak hi se koyi kiran phoot pade
zauq-e-awaargi-e-dasht-o-bayaban hi sahi
parda-e-gul hi se shayad koyi awaaz aaye
fursat-e-sair-o-tamasha-e-baharan hi sahi(4)

हासिल-ए-इश्क़ तिरा हुस्न-ए-पशेमाँ ही सही
मेरी हसरत तिरी सूरत से नुमायाँ ही सही
हुस्न भी हुस्न है मोहताज-ए-नज़र है जब तक
शो'ला-ए-इश्क़ चराग़-ए-तह-ए-दामाँ ही सही
क्या ख़बर ख़ाक ही से कोई किरन फूट पड़े
ज़ौक़-ए-आवारगी-ए-दश्त-ओ-बयाबाँ ही सही
पर्दा-ए-गुल ही से शायद कोई आवाज़ आए
फुर्सत-ए-सैर-ओ-तमाशा-ए-बहाराँ ही सही (4)

27. Let your mortified beauty be the gain of love

Let your mortified beauty be the gain of love
Let your face be a reflection of my deep love

Beauty is only when it rouses a desirous look
Though love's spark burns only under a hood

Who can tell from dust may arise a ray of light
Let me have, in desert and woods, a free flight

A voice may speak up from behind a flower
If not, let it be a leisure walk in a spring bower (4)

28. *hoti hai tere naam se vahshat kabhi kabhi*

hoti hai tere naam se vahshat kabhi kabhi
barham hui hai yun bhi tabiyat kabhi kabhi
ai dil kise nasib ye taufeeq-e-iztiraab
milti hai zindagi men ye rahat kabhi kabhi
tere karam se ai alam-e-husn-aafreen
dil ban gaya hai dost ki khalwat kabhi kabhi
josh-e-junoon men dard ki tughyaniyon ke saath
ashkon men dhal gayi teri surat kabhi kabhi (4)
tere qareeb rah ke bhi dil mutmayin na tha
guzri hai mujh pe ye bhi qayamat kabhi kabhi
kuchh apna hosh tha na tumhara khayal tha
yun bhi guzar gayi shab-e-furqat kabhi kabhi
ai dost ham ne tark-e-mohabbat ke bavajood
mahsoos ki hai teri zaroorat kabhi kabhi

होती है तेरे नाम से वहशत कभी कभी
बरहम हुई है यूँ भी तबीअत कभी कभी
ऐ दिल किसे नसीब ये तौफ़ीक़-ए-इज़्तिराब
मिलती है ज़िंदगी में ये राहत कभी कभी
तेरे करम से ऐ अलम-ए-हुस्न-आफ़रीं
दिल बन गया है दोस्त की ख़ल्वत कभी कभी
जोश-ए-जुनूँ में दर्द की तुग़्यानियों के साथ
अश्कों में ढल गई तिरी सूरत कभी कभी (4)
तेरे क़रीब रह के भी दिल मुतमइन न था
गुज़री है मुझ पे ये भी क़यामत कभी कभी
कुछ अपना होश था न तुम्हारा ख़याल था
यूँ भी गुज़र गई शब-ए-फ़ुर्क़त कभी कभी
ऐ दोस्त हम ने तर्क-ए-मोहब्बत के बावजूद
महसूस की है तेरी ज़रूरत कभी कभी

28. Your name brings revulsion at times

Your name brings revulsion at times
Leaves me frustrated with it at times

Not all hearts are worthy of restlessness
Only a few receive this bliss at times

Because of you, O my delightful pain!
Heart has become my lone mate at times

Torrents of pain in times of raging love
Find your face in drops of tears at times (4)

Even when close to you heart gets restless
I have had this disastrous feeling at times

When neither I nor you mattered any more
A night of separation like this I had at times

O my dear! even after giving up on love
I have felt your absence and need at times

29. husn ko dil men chhupa kar dekho

husn ko dil men chhupa kar dekho
dhyaan ki shama jala kar dekho
kya khabar koyi dafina mil jaye
koi deewar gira kar dekho
fakhta chup hai badi der se kyun
sarv ki shakh hila kar dekho
kyun chaman chhod diya khushbu ne
phool ke paas to ja kar dekho (4)
nahr kyun so gayi chalte chalte
koi patthar hi gira kar dekho
dil men betab hain kya kya manzar
kabhi is shahr men aa kar dekho
in andheron men kiran hai koyi
shab-e-zood aankh utha kar dekho

हुस्न को दिल में छुपा कर देखो
ध्यान की शमां जला कर देखो
क्या ख़बर कोई दफ़ीना मिल जाए
कोई दीवार गिरा कर देखो
फ़ाख़्ता चुप है बड़ी देर से क्यों
सर्व की शाख़ हिला कर देखो
क्यों चमन छोड़ दिया ख़ुशबू ने
फूल के पास तो जाकर देखो (4)
नह्र क्यों सो गयी चलते-चलते
कोई पत्थर ही गिरा कर देखो
दिल में बेताब हैं क्या-क्या मंज़र
कभी इस शहर में आकर देखो
इन अँधेरों में किरन है कोई
शब-ए-ज़ूद आँख उठा कर देखो

29. Keep secrets of beauty in your heart

Keep secrets of beauty in your heart
Keep high the flame of your thought

There may underneath lie a crown
See if you can knock a wall down

The dove for long is sitting quiet
Give the tree a shake to know why

Fragrance said the garden a goodbye
Get close to a flower to know why (4)

Running brook has stopped by and by
Throw a pebble in it to know why

Restless images are lodged in my eye
Come over my town to know why

A ray of light, darkness may hold
O night-stricken, wake up and behold

30. *in sahme huye shahron ki faza kuchh kahti hai*

in sahme huye shahron ki faza kuchh kahti hai
kabhi tum bhi suno ye dharti kya kuchh kahti hai
ye thithuri huyi lambi raaten kuchh puchhti hain
ye khamoshi-e-awaaznuma kuchh kahti hai
sab apne gharon men lambi taan ke sote hain
aur dur kahin koyal ki sadaa kuchh kahti hai
Jab subhon ko chidiyaan baari-baari bolati hain
koyi namaanoos udaas nava kuchh kahti hai (4)
jab raat ko taare baari baari jaagte hain
kayi doobe huye taron ki nida kuchh kahti hai
kabhi bhor bhaye kabhi shaam pade kabhi raat gaye
har aan badalti rut ki hava kuchh kahti hai
mehman hain ham mehmansara hai ye nagri
mehmanon ko mehmansara kuchh kahti hai
bedar raho bedar raho bedar raho
ay ham-safaro awaaz-e-dara kuchh kahti hai (8)
'nasir' ashob-e-zamana se ghafil na raho
kuchh hota hai jab khalq-e-khuda kuchh kahti hai

इन सहमे हुए शहरों की फ़ज़ा कुछ कहती है
कभी तुम भी सुनो ये धरती क्या कुछ कहती है
ये ठिठुरी हुई लम्बी रातें कुछ पूछती हैं
ये ख़ामोशी-ए-आवाज़नुमा कुछ कहती है
सब अपने घरों में लम्बी तान के सोते हैं
और दूर कहीं कोयल की सदा कुछ कहती है
जब सुब्हों को चिड़ियाँ बारी-बारी बोलती हैं
कोई नामानूस उदास नवा कुछ कहती है (4)
जब रात को तारे बारी-बारी जागते हैं
कई डूबे हुए तारों की निदा कुछ कहती है
कभी भोर भए कभी शाम पड़े कभी रात गए
हर आन बदलती रुत की हवा कुछ कहती है
मेहमान हैं हम मेहमानसरा है ये नगरी
मेहमानों को मेहमानसरा कुछ कहती है
बेदार रहो, बेदार रहो, बेदार रहो
ऐ हमसफ़रों आवाज़-ए-दरा कुछ कहती है (8)
'नासिर' आशोब-ए-ज़माना से ग़ाफ़िल न रहो
कुछ होता है जब ख़ल्क़-ए-ख़ुदा कुछ कहती है

30. The petrified state of these cities says something

The petrified state of these cities says something
Keep your ears to the ground, it says something

These long shivering nights ask for something
This eloquent voice of silence says something

People sleep in deep slumber in their homes
Far away, a cry of the cuckoo says something

When birds in the morning repeat their tweet
A strange melancholic voice says something (4)

When stars at night do their duty staying awake
The call of some shooting stars says something

At early dawn or fading evening or deep night
Breeze at every changing season says something

We are the guests and the city our housekeeper
To the guests, the housekeeper says something

Keep awake, watch out, keep awake, watch out
O my travellers, the caravan bell says something (8)

'Nasir', don't you overlook people's protestations
Something happens when public says something

31. *ishq jab zamzama-paira hoga*

ishq jab zamzama-paira hoga
husn khud mahv-e-tamasha hoga
sun ke awaaza-e-zanjeer-e-saba
qafas-e-ghuncha ka dar va hoga
daaym abad rahegi duniya
ham na honge koyi ham sa hoga
kaun dekhega tuloo-e-khurshid
zarra jab dida-e-bina hoga (4)
ham tujhe bhul ke khush baithe hain
ham sa bedard koyi kya hoga
phir sulagne laga sahra-e-khayal
abr ghir kar kahin barsa hoga

इश्क़ जब ज़मज़मा-पैरा होगा
हुस्न ख़ुद महव-ए-तमाशा होगा
सुन के आवाज़ा-ए-ज़ंजीर-ए-सबा
क़फ़स-ए-ग़ुंचा का दर वा होगा
दाइम आबाद रहेगी दुनिया
हम न होंगे कोई हम सा होगा
कौन देखेगा तुलू-ए-ख़ुर्शीद
ज़र्रा जब दीदा-ए-बीना होगा (4)
हम तुझे भूल के ख़ुश बैठे हैं
हम सा बेदर्द कोई क्या होगा
फिर सुलगने लगा सहरा-ए-ख़याल
अब्र घिर कर कहीं बरसा होगा

--continue--

31. When love sings in all its resplendence

When love sings in all its resplendence
Beauty stands mesmerised in its attendance

On hearing the ringing footsteps of a breeze
Doors of the trapped blossoms did release

For times to come the world is here to stay
If not us, others like us will have their day

Who on earth will look up to the rising Sun
When every dust particle will shine like one (4)

After forgetting about you I am sitting pretty
Can you imagine someone as pitiless as me?

Glowing embers rise up in my arid imagination
Far away, a cloud must have burst in profusion
--continue--

31. ishq jab zamzama-paira hoga

phir kisi dhyaan ke sad-rahe par
dil-e-hairatzada tanha hoga
phir kisi subah-e-tarab ka jaadu
parda-e-shab se huvaida hoga (8)
ik sada sang men tadpi hogi
ik sharar phool men larza hoga
tujh ko har phool men uryan sote
chandni raat ne dekha hoga
dekh kar aina-e-aab-e-ravan
patta patta lab-e-goya hoga
shaam se soch raha hun 'nasir'
chand kis shahr men utra hoga (12)

फिर किसी ध्यान के सद-राहे पर
दिल-ए-हैरत-ज़दा तन्हा होगा
फिर किसी सुब्ह-ए-तरब का जादू
पर्दा-ए-शब से हुवैदा होगा (8)
इक सदा संग में तड़पी होगी
इक शरर फूल में लर्ज़ां होगा
तुझ को हर फूल में उर्याँ सोते
चाँदनी-रात ने देखा होगा
देख कर आइना-ए-आब-ए-रवाँ
पत्ता पत्ता लब-ए-गोया होगा
शाम से सोच रहा हूँ 'नासिर'
चाँद किस शहर में उतरा होगा (12)

31. When love sings in all its resplendence

At the crossroads of a thousand thought-stream
The heart stands alone, bewildered in a dream

A sudden magic of a morning full of delight
Will rise up from behind the curtain of a night (8)

A cry would have caused a rock to tremor
A fire spark would have lurked in a flower

While you were sleeping naked in every flower
The moonlit night espied you despite the cover

On watching the mirror of a running stream
Leaves like lips went on chattering full steam

Since evening 'Nasir' has been contemplating
Which town the moon will now be dating (12)

32. *ishq men jeet huyi ya maat*

ishq men jeet huyi yaa maat
aaj ki raat na chhed ye baat
yun aaya vo jaan-e-bahar
jaise jag men phaile baat
rang khule sahra ki dhoop
zulf ghane jangal ki raat
kuchh n suna aur kuchh na kaha
dil men rah gayi dil ki baat (4)
yaar ki nagari koson door
kaise kategi bhaari raat
basti vaalon se chhup kar
ro lete hain pichhali raat
sannaton men sunate hain
suni-sunaai koyi baat

इश्क़ में जीत हुई या मात
आज की रात न छेड़ ये बात
यूँ आया वो जान-ए-बहार
जैसे जग में फैले बात
रंग, खुले सहरा की धूप
ज़ुल्फ़ घने जंगल की रात
कुछ न सुना और कुछ न कहा
दिल में रह गयी दिल की बात (4)
यार की नगरी कोसों दूर
कैसे कटेगी भारी रात
बस्ती वालों से छुपकर
रो लेते हैं पिछली रात
सन्नाटों में सुनते हैं
सुनी-सुनाई कोई बात

32. In love, did you lose or gain?

In love, did you lose or gain?
Tonight, don't talk about it again

Thus came my love in springtide
Like rumour spreads far and wide

Like the sun in a desert, she was fair
A nightly jungle darkness in her hair

Nothing was heard, nothing said
All remained tied up in the head (4)

Lover's abode is many a mile away
A long night ahead, nowhere to stay

Hiding from the neighbour's sight
We cry in silence late at night

In the still darkness of night, we hear
Stories told and heard everywhere

33. *is se pahle ki bichhad jaayen ham*

is se pahle ki bichhad jaayen ham
do-qadam aur mere saath chalo
abhi dekha nahin jee bhar ke tumhen
abhi kuchh der mere paas raho
mujh sa phir koyi na aayega yahan
rok lo mujh ko agar rok sako
yun na guzregi shab-e-gham 'nasir'
us ki ankhon ki kahani chhedo (4)

इस से पहले कि बिछड़ जाएँ हम
दो-क़दम और मिरे साथ चलो
अभी देखा नहीं जी-भर के तुम्हें
अभी कुछ देर मिरे पास रहो
मुझ सा फिर कोई न आएगा यहाँ
रोक लो मुझ को अगर रोक सको
यूँ न गुज़रेगी शब-ए-ग़म 'नासिर'
उस की आँखों की कहानी छेड़ो (4)

33. Before we decide to split forever

Before we decide to split forever
Let's take a few more steps together

I haven't had my heart's fill of you yet
For some more time with me, stay hither

You won't find again another like me
Hold me back if you can, right here

The night of suffering won't end 'Nasir'
Let's talk about her eyes, it is better

34. jabin pe dhoop si ankhon men kuchh haya si hai

jabin pe dhoop si ankhon men kuchh haya si hai
tu ajnabi hai magar shakl aashna si hai
khayal hi nahin aata kisi musibat ka
tere khayal men har baat gham-ruba si hai
jahan men yun to kise chain hai magar pyare
ye tere phool se chehre pe kyun udaasi hai
dil-e-garmin se bhi jalte hain shadman-e-hayat
usi charagh ki ab shahr men hava si hai (4)
hamin se aankh churaata hai us ka har zarra
magar ye khaak hamare hi khoon ki pyaasi hai
udaas phirta hun main jis ki dhun men barson se
yunhi si hai vo khushi baat vo zara si hai
chahakte bolte shahron ko kya hua 'nasir'
ki din ko bhi mere ghar men vahi udaasi hai

जबीं पे धूप सी आँखों में कुछ हया सी है
तू अजनबी है मगर शक्ल आश्ना सी है
ख़याल ही नहीं आता किसी मुसीबत का
तिरे ख़याल में हर बात ग़म-रुबा सी है
जहाँ में यूँ तो किसे चैन है मगर प्यारे
ये तेरे फूल से चेहरे पे क्यूँ उदासी है
दिल-ए-गर्मीं से भी जलते हैं शादमान-ए-हयात
उसी चराग़ की अब शहर में हवा सी है (4)
हमीं से आँख चुराता है उस का हर ज़र्रा
मगर ये ख़ाक हमारे ही ख़ूँ की प्यासी है
उदास फिरता हूँ मैं जिस की धुन में बरसों से
यूँही सी है वो ख़ुशी बात वो ज़रा सी है
चहकते बोलते शहरों को क्या हुआ 'नासिर'
कि दिन को भी मिरे घर में वही उदासी है

34. Those sunny eyes on your face have some coyness

Those sunny eyes on your face have some coyness
A stranger you are, but there's a hint of friendliness

Reminiscing about you, I can't think of any misery
A thought of you is like someone robbing my agony

I know, my dear, in this world no one is at peace
But why have despair on your flower like face?

Warmth of heart too can light up life with gaiety
Such lamps are much in demand now in the city (4)

Every dust-particle avoids eye contact with us
Though the same dust seems blood-thirsty for us

For years what I have been looking for sadly
Is something trivial - a bit of happiness actually

What happened 'Nasir' to the bustling towns
Even daytime, our homes wear the same frowns

35. *jab zara tez hava hoti hai*

jab zara tez hava hoti hai
kaisi sunsaan faza hoti hai
ham ne dekhe hain vo sannate bhi
jab har ik saans sadaa hoti hai
dil ka ye haal huya tere baad
jaise viraansara hoti hai
rona aata hai hamen bhi lekin
is men tauheen-e-wafa hoti hai (4)
munh-andhere kabhi uth kar dekho
kya tar-o-taaza hava hoti hai
ajnabi dhyaan ki har mauj ke saath
kis qadar tez hava hoti hai
gham ki benoor guzargahon men
ik kiran zauq-faza hoti hai

जब ज़रा तेज़ हवा होती है
कैसी सुनसान फ़ज़ा होती है
हमने देखे हैं वो सन्नाटे भी
जब हर इक साँस सदा होती है
दिल का ये हाल हुआ तेरे बाद
जैसे वीरानसरा होती है
रोना आता है हमें भी लेकिन
इसमें तौहीन-ए-वफ़ा होती है (4)
मुँह अँधेरे कभी उठ कर देखो
क्या तर-ओ-ताज़ा हवा होती है
अजनबी ध्यान की हर मौज के साथ
किस क़दर तेज़ हवा होती है
ग़म की बेनूर गुज़रगाहों में
इक किरन ज़ौक़-फ़ज़ा होती है

--continue--

35. When there is that fierce wind

When there is that fierce wind
How quiet the all-around is

We have seen that dark stillness,
When every breath a scream is

After you left, my heart felt
Like a deserted house that it is

I can cry too but know that
How humiliating for love it is (4)

Get up early morning and see,
How fresh and balmy the air is

Breezing through strange thoughts
I find how quick the airstream is

On the unlit highways of sorrow
How blissful a solitary ray is
              --continue--

35. jab zara tez hava hoti hai

gham-gusar-e-safar-e-raah-e-wafa
mizha-e-aabla-paa hoti hai (8)
gulshan-e-fikr ki munh-band kali
shab-e-mahtab men va hoti hai
jab nikalti hai nigar-e-shab-e-gul
munh pe shabnam ki rida hoti hai
hadsa hai ki khizan se pahle
boo-e-gul gul se juda hoti hai
ik naya daur janam leta hai
ek tahzeeb fana hoti hai (12)
jab koyi gham nahin hota 'nasir'
bekali dil ka siva hoti hai

ग़मगुसार-ए-सफ़र-ए-राह-ए-वफ़ा
मिज़ा-ए-आबला-पा होती है (8)
गुलशन-ए-फ़िक्र की मुँहबंद कली
शब-ए-महताब में वा होती है
जब निकलती है निगार-ए-शब-ए-गुल
मुँह पे शबनम की रिदा होती है
हादसा है कि ख़िज़ाँ से पहले
बू-ए-गुल गुल से जुदा होती है
इक नया दौर जनम लेता है
एक तहज़ीब फ़ना होती है (12)
जब कोई ग़म नहीं होता 'नासिर'
बेकली दिल का सिवा होती है

35. When there is that fierce wind

Walkers on the rough road of love
Know how blistered their foot is (8)

A budding idea in mind's garden
Opens up when moonlit the night is

The beauty of a night flower shows
When wrapped in dew it is

Before autumn, the fragrance
Leaves the flower, how tragic it is

A new age prospers on the death
Of old, that is the way world is (12)

When 'Nasir' has no sorrows
An agitated heart is what he is

36. *Jalwa-saaman hai rang-o-boo ham se*

jalwa-saaman hai rang-o-boo ham se
is chaman ki hai aabroo ham se
dars lete hain khush-khirami ka
mauj-e-dariya-o-aab-joo ham se
har sahar baargah-e-shabnam men
phool milte hain ba-vazoo ham se
ham se roshan hai kargaah-e-sukhan
nafas-e-gul hai mushkboo ham se (4)
shab ki tanhaiyon men pichhle pahar
chand karta hai guftugoo ham se
shahr men ab hamare charche hain
jagmagate hain kakh-o-koo ham se

जल्वा-सामाँ है रंग-ओ-बू हम से
इस चमन की है आबरू हम से
दर्स लेते हैं ख़ुश-ख़िरामी का
मौज-ए-दरिया-ओ-आब-जू हम से
हर सहर बारगाह-ए-शबनम में
फूल मिलते हैं बा-वज़ू हम से
हम से रौशन है कार-गाह-ए-सुख़न
नफ़स-ए-गुल है मुश्कबू हम से (4)
शब की तन्हाइयों में पिछले पहर
चाँद करता है गुफ़्तुगू हम से
शहर में अब हमारे चर्चे हैं
जगमगाते हैं काख़-ओ-कू हम से

36. Colour and smell owe their glory to us

Colour and smell owe their glory to us
The garden owes its reputation to us

The waves of river, the running brooks
Take lesson in graceful flow from us

Every morning in the presence of dew
Freshly washed flowers run into us

We have lighted the workplace of poetry
Flowers breathe of musk due to us (4)

In the late hours of a solitary night
The moon gets to talking with us

All around we are the talk of the town
The palaces and lanes are abuzz with us

37. *jo guftni nahin vo baat bhi sunaa dunga*

jo guftni nahin vo baat bhi sunaa dunga
tu ek baar to mil sab gile mita dunga
majaal hai koyi mujhse tujhe judaa kar de
jahan bhi jayega tu main tujhe sadaa dunga
teri gali men bahut der se khada hun magar
kisi ne poochh liya to jawaab kya dunga
meri khamosh nigahon ko chashme-kam se na dekh
main ro pada to dilon ke tabak hilaa dunga (4)
yun hi udaas raha main to dekhna ik din
tamaam shahr men tanhaiyaan bichha dunga
ba-paase-sohbate-derina koyi baat hi kar
nazar milaa to sahi, main tujhe dua dunga
bulaaonga na milunga, na khat likhunga tujhe
teri khushi ke liye khud ko ye sazaa dunga
vo dard hi na raha varna ai mataa-e-hayaat
mujhe gumaan bhi na tha main tujhe bhula dunga (8)
abhi to raat hai kuch der so hi le 'nasir'
koyi bulaayega to main tujhe jaga dunga.

जो गुफ्तनी नहीं वो बात भी सुना दूंगा
तू एक बार तो मिल सब गिले मिटा दूंगा
मजाल है कोई मुझसे तुझे जुदा कर दे
जहां भी जायेगा तू मैं तुझे सदा दूंगा
तेरी गली में बहुत देर से खड़ा हूँ मगर
किसी ने पूछ लिया तो जवाब क्या दूंगा
मेरी खमोश निगाहों को चश्मे-कम से न देख
मैं रो पड़ा तो दिलों के तबक़ हिला दूंगा (4)
यूँ ही उदास रहा मैं तो देखना इक दिन
तमाम शहर में तन्हाईयाँ बिछा दूंगा
ब-पासे-सोहबते-देरीना कोई बात ही कर
नज़र मिला तो सही, मैं तुझे दुआ दूंगा
बुलाऊंगा न मिलूंगा, न ख़त लिखूंगा तुझे
तेरी खुशी के लिए खुद को ये सज़ा दूंगा
वो दर्द ही न रहा वरना ऐ मता-ए-हयात
मुझे गुमां भी न था मैं तुझे भुला दूंगा (8)
अभी तो रात है कुछ देर सो ही ले 'नासिर'
कोई बुलायेगा तो मैं तुझे जगा दूंगा।

37. I'll speak what I am not supposed to speak

I'll speak what I am not supposed to speak
Once we meet, you'll hear all that you seek

How dare anyone tear you away from me
Wherever you are, you will hear me speak

For too long I have been waiting in your lane
If someone questions me what shall I speak

Don't judge my dry eyes with a look of scorn
I can rend hearts with tears and a high shriek (4)

If this sorrow lingers on, you will see one day
How into the entire city loneliness will sneak

For the sake of old times, do say something
Look into my eyes, a prayer for you I'll read

I will not call or meet you, nor write to you
For your sake, this ordeal upon me I'll wreak

The pain that once was my boon has passed
Else, chances of forgetting you were bleak (8)

You can sleep for a while 'Nasir', it's still dark
If someone calls you, I will give you a beep

38. *jurm-e-inkar ki sazaa hi de*

*jurm-e-inkar ki sazaa hi de
mere haq men bhi kuchh sunaa hi de
ishq men ham nahin ziyada talab
jo tera naaz-e-kam-nigaahi de
tu ne taaron se shab ki maang bhari
mujh ko ik ashk-e-subah-gaahi de
tu ne banjar zamin ko phool diye
mujh ko ik zakhm-e-dil-kushaa hi de (4)
bastiyon ko diye hain tu ne charagh
dasht-e-dil ko bhi koyi raahi de
umr bhar ki nava-gari ka sila
ai khuda koyi ham-navaa hi de
zard-roo hain varaq khayalon ke
ai shab-e-hijr kuchh syaahi de
gar majal-e-sukhan nahin 'nasir'
lab-e-khamosh se gavaahi de (8)*

जुर्म-ए- इनकार की सज़ा ही दे
मेरे हक़ में भी कुछ सुना ही दे
इश्क़ में हम नहीं ज़ियादा तलब
जो तिरा नाज़-ए-कम-निगाही दे
तू ने तारों से शब की माँग भरी
मुझ को इक अश्क-ए-सुब्ह-गाही दे
तू ने बंजर ज़मीं को फूल दिए
मुझ को इक ज़ख़्म-ए-दिल-कुशा ही दे (4)
बस्तियों को दिए हैं तू ने चराग़
दश्त-ए-दिल को भी कोई राही दे
उम्र भर की नवा-गरी का सिला
ऐ ख़ुदा कोई हम-नवा ही दे
ज़र्द-रू हैं वरक़ ख़यालों के
ऐ शब-ए-हिज्र कुछ स्याही दे
गर मजाल-ए-सुख़न नहीं 'नासिर'
लब-ए-ख़ामोश से गवाही दे (8)

38. For saying no, order a punishment for me

For saying no, order a punishment for me
In favour too, do say something for me

I do not look for much in return for love
Give whatever little you can spare for me

You have adorned the nights with stars
For my mornings, endorse a tear for me

You have ordained flowers to barren land
Grant me a lesion that slits heart for me (4)

To town dwellers you have provided light
For heart's darkness, a torchbearer for me

As a recompense to my life-long crooning
God, provide a good accompanist for me

Pale blank are the sheets of my muse
O night of separation, ink them for me

Unable if I am to write a poem 'Nasir'
Make my silent lips a witness for me (8)

39. *kab talak muddaa kahe koyi*

kab talak muddaa kahe koyi
na suno tum to kya kahe koyi
ghairat-e-ishq ko kubool nahin
ki tujhe bewafa kahe koyi
minnat-e-nakhuda nahin manzoor
chahe us ko khuda kahe koyi
har koyi apne gham men hai masroof
kis ko dard-ashna kahe koyi(4)
kaun achha hai is zamaane men
kyun kisi ko bura kahe koyi
koyi to haq-shanaas ho ya rab
zulm ko naravaa kahe koyi
vo na samjhenge in kinayon ko
jo kahe barmala kahe koyi
aarzoo hai ki mera qissa-e-shauq
aaj mere siva kahe koyi (8)
jee men aata hai kuchh kahun 'nasir'
kya khabar sun ke kya kahe koyi

कब तलक मुद्दआ कहे कोई
न सुनो तुम तो क्या कहे कोई
ग़ैरत-ए-इश्क़ को क़बूल नहीं
कि तुझे बेवफ़ा कहे कोई
मिन्नत-ए-नाख़ुदा नहीं मंज़ूर
चाहे उसको ख़ुदा कहे कोई
हर कोई अपने ग़म में है मसरूफ़
किसको दर्द-आशना कहे कोई (4)
कौन अच्छा है इस ज़माने में
क्यों किसी को बुरा कहे कोई
कोई तो हक़-शनास हो या रब
ज़ुल्म को नारवा कहे कोई
वो न समझेंगे इन किनायों को
जो कहे बरमला कहे कोई
आरज़ू है कि मेरा क़िस्सा-ए-शौक़
आज मेरे सिवा कहे कोई (8)
जी में आता है कुछ कहूँ 'नासिर'
क्या ख़बर सुन के क्या कहे कोई

39. How long can one insist on his say

How long can one insist on his say
If you don't listen, what can one say

For the honour of love I cannot accept
'You are unfaithful' if anyone dare say

No way can I submit to the boatman*
Even if he is God as someone may say

Everyone is reeling in their own misery
Who knows real pain, no one can say (4)

Can we tell who is good in this world?
That someone is bad why one should say

O god, someone must speak up for rights
And 'repression is not right' dare say

I am sure they would not take these hints
We have to say directly, whatever we say

I wish someone else today takes over
The story of my faith and gives it a say (8)

I think I should say something 'Nasir'
But, after what I hear, what can one say?

*boatman in Urdu is called 'nakhuda' which includes the word 'khuda' (God).

40. kal jinhen zindagi thi raas bahut

kal jinhen zindagi thi raas bahut
aaj dekha unhen udaas bahut
raftagan ka nishan nahin milta
ug rahi hai zamin pe ghaas bahut
kyun na roun teri judaai men
din guzaare hain tere paas bahut
chhanv mil jaaye daman-e-gul ki
hai gharibi men ye libaas bahut (4)
vaadi-e-dil men paanv dekh ke rakh
hai yahan dard ki ugaas bahut
sukhe patton ko dekh kar 'nasir'
yaad aati hai gul ki baas bahut

कल जिन्हें ज़िन्दगी थी रास बहुत
आज देखा उन्हें उदास बहुत
रफ़्तगाँ का निशाँ नहीं मिलता
उग रही है ज़मीं पे घास बहुत
क्यों न रोऊँ तिरी जुदाई में
दिन गुज़ारे हैं तेरे पास बहुत
छाँव मिल जाए दामन-ए-गुल की
है ग़रीबी में ये लिबास बहुत (4)
वादी-ए-दिल में पाँव देख के रख
है यहाँ दर्द की उगास बहुत
सूखे पत्तों को देखकर 'नासिर'
याद आती है गुल की बास बहुत

40. Yesterday, those who rejoiced in life

Yesterday, those who rejoiced in life
Today have come to much strife

No footprints of those who left us
Overgrown is ground, the grass is rife

Why should I not cry on parting
What good days we had in life

If one gets shade of a flower-bough
What a cover it is for poor life   (4)

Careful, when you step into the heart
It is a valley of grief and pain in life

When I look at dead petals 'Nasir'
I get that scent when lowers had life

41. *kaarvan sust rahbar khamosh*

kaarvan sust rahbar khamosh
kaise guzrega ye safar khamosh
tujhe kahna hai kuchh magar khamosh
dekh aur dekh kar guzar khamosh
yun tere raste men baitha hun
jaise ik sham-e-rahguzar khamosh
tu jahan ek baar aaya tha
ek muddat se hai vo ghar khamosh (4)
us gali ke guzarne valon ko
takte rahte hain bam-o-dar khamosh
uth gaye kaise kaise pyare log
ho gaye kaise kaise ghar khamosh

कारवाँ सुस्त राहबर ख़ामोश
कैसे गुज़रेगा ये सफ़र ख़ामोश
तुझे कहना है कुछ मगर ख़ामोश
देख और देख कर गुज़र ख़ामोश
यूँ तिरे रास्ते में बैठा हूँ
जैसे इक शम-ए-रहगुज़र ख़ामोश
तू जहाँ एक बार आया था
एक मुद्दत से है वो घर ख़ामोश (4)
उस गली के गुज़रने वालों को
तकते रहते हैं बाम-ओ-दर ख़ामोश
उठ गए कैसे कैसे प्यारे लोग
हो गए कैसे कैसे घर ख़ामोश
--coninue--

41. Caravan sluggish, the guide in silence

Caravan sluggish, the guide in silence
How'd we make this journey in silence

'Want to say something?' better not
Take a look, and pass by in silence

I am sitting in the middle of your way
Like a lighted street lamp in silence

The house that you visited once
Has been for long lying in silence (4)

All those passersby in that lane are
Watched over from rooftops in silence

How many dear ones have we lost
How many homes turned into silence
      --continue--

41. kaarvan sust rahbar khamosh

ye zamin kis ke intizar men hai
kya khabar kyun hai ye nagar khamosh
shahr sota hai raat jaati hai
koyi toofan hai parda-dar khamosh (8)
ab ke beda guzar gaya to kya
hain abhi kitne hi bhanvar khamosh
chadhte dariya ka dar nahin yaaro
main hun sahil ko dekh kar khamosh
abhi vo qafile nahin aaye
abhi baithen na hamsafar khamosh
har-nafas ik payam tha 'nasir'
ham hi baithe rahe magar khamosh (12)

ये ज़मीं किस के इंतिज़ार में है
क्या ख़बर क्यूँ है ये नगर ख़ामोश
शहर सोता है रात जाती है
कोई तूफ़ाँ है पर्दा-दर ख़ामोश (8)
अब के बेड़ा गुज़र गया तो क्या
हैं अभी कितने ही भँवर ख़ामोश
चढ़ते दरिया का डर नहीं यारो
मैं हूँ साहिल को देख कर ख़ामोश
अभी वो क़ाफ़िले नहीं आए
अभी बैठें न हम-सफ़र ख़ामोश
हर-नफ़स इक पयाम था 'नासिर'
हम ही बैठे रहे मगर ख़ामोश (12)

41. Caravan sluggish, the guide in silence

What does this land stand in wait for
Any clue, why the city is in silence?

City sleeps while the night moves on
A storm is brewing in the dark silence (8)

Even if we get the boat across this time
Many a swirls lie ahead in silence

I am not much scared of the rising river
It is the bank I am looking at in silence

Those caravans have not yet arrived
Until then, mates, don't rest in silence

Every moment was a kind of signal 'Nasir'
It was we who kept idling in silence (12)

42. kaun is raah se guzarta hai

kaun is raah se guzarta hai
dil yun hi intizar karta hai
dekh kar bhi na dekhne vaale
dil tujhe dekh dekh darta hai
shahr-e-gul men kati hai saari raat
dekhiye din kahan guzarta hai
dhyaan ki sidhiyon pe pichhle pahar
koyi chupke se paanv dharta hai (4)
dil to mera udaas hai 'nasir'
shahr kyun saaen saaen karta hai

कौन इस राह से गुज़रता है
दिल यूँ ही इन्तज़ार करता है
देखकर भी न देखने वाले
दिल तुझे देख-देख डरता है
शहर-ए-गुल में कटी है सारी रात
देखिए दिन कहाँ गुज़रता है
ध्यान की सीढ़ियों पे पिछले पहर
कोई चुपके से पाँव धरता है (4)
दिल तो मेरा उदास है 'नासिर'
शहर क्यों साँय-साँय करता है

42. Who, I guess, will pass by this lane

Who, I guess, will pass by this lane
The heart though waits in vain

You, who look but don't see,
Make me nervous when you I see

At night, I was in a flower-laden city
See what the day has in store for me

In the late hours of a brooding night
Someone moves in with a step light (4)

'Nasir' I know my heart feels miserable
But why does the city look so dismal

43. *khayal-e-tark-e-tamanna na kar sake tu bhi*

khayal-e-tark-e-tamanna na kar sake tu bhi
udaasiyon ka mudaava na kar sake tu bhi
kabhi vo vaqt bhi aaye ke koyi lamha-e-aish
mere baghair gavaara na kar sake tu bhi
khuda vo din na dikhaye tujhe ki meri tarah
meri vafa pe bharosa na kar sake tu bhi
main apna uqda-e-dil tujh ko saump deta hun
bada maza ho agar va na kar sake tu bhi (4)
tujhe ye gham ki meri zindagi ka kya hoga
mujhe ye zid ki mudaava na kar sake tu bhi
na kar khayal-e-talafi ke mera zakhm-e-wafa
vo zakhm hai jise achchha na kar sake tu bhi

ख़याल-ए-तर्क़-ए-तमन्ना न कर सके तू भी
उदासियों का मुदावा न कर सके तू भी
कभी वो वक़्त भी आए कि कोई लम्हा-ए-ऐश
मिरे बग़ैर गवारा न कर सके तू भी
ख़ुदा वो दिन न दिखाये तुझे कि मेरी तरह
मेरी वफ़ा पे भरोसा न कर सके तू भी
मैं अपना उक़्दा-ए-दिल तुझको सौंप देता हूँ
बड़ा मज़ा हो अगर वा न कर सके तू भी (4)
तुझे ये ग़म कि मेरी ज़िंदगी का क्या होगा
मुझे ये ज़िद कि मुदावा न कर सके तू भी
न कर ख़याल-ए-तलाफ़ी कि मेरा ज़ख़्म-ए-वफ़ा
वो ज़ख़्म है जिसे अच्छा न कर सके तू भी

43. Hope you too won't give up on your passion

Hope you too won't give up on your passion
And find no relief to your state of depression

Hope there comes a time when you too will be
Unable to relish a happy moment without me

Hope, like me, you wouldn't run into a time
When you too would mistrust my love sublime

I would gladly present my locked heart to you
What fun, if you'd not be able to open it too (4)

You worry about what my life and fate will be
I will ensure that you too bring no relief to me

Don't you try to heal injury of my heartbreak
It is such a repair that even you cannot make

44. kise dekhen kahan dekha na jaaye

kise dekhen kahan dekha na jaaye
vo dekha hai jahan dekha na jaaye
meri barbaadiyon pe rone vaale
tujhe mahv-e-fugan dekha na jaaye
zameen logon se khaali ho rahi hai
ye rang-e-aasman dekha na jaaye
safar hai aur gurbat ka safar hai
gham-e-sad-kaarvan dekha na jaaye (4)
kahin aag aur kahin laashon ke ambaar
bas ai daur-e-zaman dekha na jaaye
dar-o-deewar veeran, shama maddham
shab-e-gham kaa saman dekha na jaaye
puraani suhabaten yaad aa rahi hain
charaagon kaa dhuaan dekha na jaaye
kahin tum aur kahin ham, kyaa gazab hai
firaaq-e-jism-o-jaan dekha na jaaye (8)
vo hi jo haasil-e-hasti hai 'nasir'
usee ko mehraban dekha n jaaye

किसे देखें कहाँ देखा न जाये
वो देखा है जहाँ देखा न जाये
मिरी बर्बादियों पे रोने वाले
तुझे मह्व-ए-फ़ुग़ाँ देखा न जाये
ज़मीं लोगों से ख़ाली हो रही है
ये रंग-ए-आसमाँ देखा न जाये
सफ़र है और ग़ुरबत का सफ़र है
ग़म-ए-सद-कारवाँ देखा न जाये (4)
कहीं आग और कहीं लाशों के अंबार
बस ऐ दौर-ए-ज़माँ देखा न जाये
दर-ओ-दीवार वीराँ, शम्अ मद्धम
शब-ए-ग़म का समाँ देखा न जाये
पुरानी सुहबतें याद आ रही हैं
चिराग़ों का धुआँ देखा न जाये
कहीं तुम और कहीं हम, क्या ग़ज़ब है
फ़िराक़-ए-जिस्म-ओ-जाँ देखा न जाये (8)
वो ही जो हासिल-ए-हस्ती है 'नासिर'
उसी को मेहबाँ देखा न जाये

44. Where can I look for who I can't see

Where can I look for who I can't see
I have seen that what we can't see

You who cried with me in my misery
Your misery in suffering, I can't see

Land getting deserted People dying
This mood of the heaven, I can't see

It is a journey and a journey in exile
This cavalcade of misery I can't see (4)

Fire in here, heaps of corpses there
Alas! these horrible times, I can't see

Home with barren walls and dim lights
This sight of agonizing night, I can't see

Images of old gatherings flash back
The smoke of dying candles, I can't see

How strange, here I am and you there
The body apart from soul, I can't see (8)

That, who is the sole bliss of life, 'Nasir'
is the one, my dearest, who I can't see

45. kisi ka dard ho dil beqaraar apna hai

kisi ka dard ho dil beqaraar apna hai
hava kahin ki ho seena figaar apna hai
ho koyi fasl magar zakhm khil hi jaate hain
sadabahar dil-e-daghdaar apna hai
bala se ham na piyen maikada to garm hua
baqadr-e-trishnagi ranj-e-khumaar apna hai
jo shaad phirte the kal aaj chhup ke rote hain
hazaar shukr gham-e-payedaar apna hai (4)
isi liye yahan kuchh log ham se jalte hain
ki jee jalane men kyun ikhtiyaar apna hai
na tang kar dil-e-mahzun ko ai gham-e-duniya
khudai bhar men yahi ghamgusaar apna hai
kahin mila to kisi din manaa hi lenge use
vo zud-ranj sahi phir bhi yaar apna hai
vo koyi apne siva ho to uska shikva karun
judai apni hai aur intizaar apna hai (8)
na dhundh 'nasir'-e-ashufta-hal ko ghar men
vo boo-e-gul ki tarah beqaraar apna hai

किसी का दर्द हो, दिल बेक़रार अपना है
हवा कहीं की हो सीना फ़िगार अपना है
हो कोई फ़स्ल मगर ज़ख़्म खिल ही जाते हैं
सदाबहार दिल-ए-दाग़दार अपना है
बला से हम न पिएँ मैकदा तो गर्म हुआ
बक़द्र-ए-तश्नगी रंज-ए-ख़ुमार अपना है
जो शाद फिरते थे कल आज छुप के रोते हैं
हज़ार शुक्र ग़म-ए-पायदार अपना है (4)
इसीलिए यहाँ कुछ लोग हमसे जलते हैं
कि जी जलाने में क्यों इख़्तियार अपना है
न तंग कर दिल-ए-महजूँ को ए ग़म-ए-दुनिया
खुदाई भर में यही ग़मगुसार अपना है
कहीं मिला तो किसी दिन मना ही लेंगे उसे
वो जूद-रंज सही फिर भी यार अपना है
वो कोई अपने सिवा हो तो उसका शिकवा करूँ
जुदाई अपनी है और इन्तज़ार अपना है (8)
न ढूँढ 'नासिर'-ए-आशुफ़्ता-हाल को घर में
वो बू-ए-गुल की तरह बेक़रार अपना है

45. Whoever is in pain, my heart goes into unrest

Whoever is in pain, my heart goes into unrest
Winds of change, if any, tear into my chest

Whatever the season, I get a good crop of hurts
My heart remains evergreen with scars at best

Whether I drink or not, good the tavern is full
I savour the high of sorrow as drinker his thirst

Those who were in good cheer cry in secret now
Mercifully, my pain is everlsting, takes no rest (4)

Many a people burn up with me because of it
The sole right to scorch my heart that I wrest

Sorrows of the world! Don't pester my heart
It is the only secret-sharer on earth I can trust

The day we run into each other, we will patch up
He may be bitter now, but we are friends closest

I can't complain as he is no other but a part of me
Parted we may be, but still wait for him I must (8)

Try not to find that woe-be-gone 'Nasir' at home
Like the fragrance of a flower he is never at rest

46. kisi kali ne bhi dekha na aankh bhar ke mujhe

Kisi kali ne bhi dekha na aankh bhar ke mujhe
guzar gayi jaras-e-gul udaas kar ke mujhe
main so raha tha kisi yaad ke shabistan men
jaga ke chhod gaye qafile sahar ke mujhe
main ro raha tha muqaddar ki sakht rahon men
uda ke le gaye jaadu teri nazar ke mujhe
main tere dard ki tughyaniyon men doob gaya
pukarte rahe taare ubhar ubhar ke mujhe (4)
tere firaq ki raaten kabhi na bhulengi
maze mile unhin raaton men umr bhar ke mujhe
zara si der thaharne de ai gham-e-duniya
bula raha hai koyi baam se utar ke mujhe
phir aaj aayi thee ik mauja-e-hava-e-tarab
suna gayi hai fasane idhar udhar ke mujhe

किसी कली ने भी देखा न आँख भर के मुझे
गुज़र गयी जरस-ए-गुल उदास करके मुझे
मैं सो रहा था किसी याद के शबिस्ताँ में
जगा के छोड़ गये क़ाफ़िले सहर के मुझे
मैं रो रहा था मुक़द्दर की सख़्त राहों में
उड़ा के ले गये जादू तिरी नज़र के मुझे
मैं तेरे दर्द की तुग़ियानियों में डूब गया
पुकारते रहे तारे उभर-उभर के मुझे (4)
तिरे फ़िराक़ की रातें कभी न भूलेंगी
मज़े मिले इन्हीं रातों में उम्र भर के मुझे
ज़रा-सी देर ठहरने दे ऐ ग़म-ए-दुनिया
बुला रहा है कोई बाम से उतर के मुझे
फिर आज आई थी इक मौज-ए-हवा-ए-तरब
सुना गयी है फ़साने इधर-उधर के मुझे

46. No look of longing from a new blossom for me

No look of longing from a new blossom for me
Convoys of spring came but only saddened me

Asleep I was in the bed chamber of a memory
Came the cavalcade of morning and shook me

Lost, I was crying on the rough roads of fate
With your bewitching gaze off you swept me

I sank down in the high tide of your torment
Though stars kept reassuring and uplifting me (4)

Never will I forget the nights of your separation
They gave pleasure indeed of a lifetime to me

Give me a little break, O worries of the world!
Rushing down the rooftop, someone is calling me

A whiff of happiness came visiting again today
Told itsy bitsy stories from here and there to me

47. kuchh to ehsas-e-ziyan tha pahle

kuchh to ehsas-e-ziyan tha pahle
dil ka ye haal kahan tha pahle
ab to jhonke se laraz uthta hun
nashsha-e-khwab-e-giran tha pahle
ab to manzil bhi hai khud garm-e-safar
har qadam sang-e-nishan tha pahle
safar-e-shauq ke farsang na poochh
waqt be-qaid makan tha pahle (4)
ye alag baat ki gham raas hai ab
us men andesha-e-jaan tha pahle
yun na ghabrae huye phirte the
dil ajab kunj-e-aman tha pahle
ab bhi tu paas nahin hai lekin
is qadar door kahan tha pahle
dere daale hain bagulon ne jahan
us taraf chashma ravaan tha pahle (8)
ab vo dariya na vo basti na vo log
kya khabar kaun kahan tha pahle

कुछ तो एहसास-ए-ज़ियाँ था पहले
दिल का ये हाल कहाँ था पहले
अब तो झोंके से लरज़ उठता हूँ
नश्शा-ए-ख़्वाब-ए-गिराँ था पहले
अब तो मंज़िल भी है ख़ुद गर्म-ए-सफ़र
हर क़दम संग-ए-निशाँ था पहले
सफ़र-ए-शौक़ के फ़रसंग न पूछ
वक़्त बे-क़ैद मकाँ था पहले (4)
ये अलग बात कि ग़म रास है अब
उस में अंदेशा-ए-जाँ था पहले
यूँ न घबराए हुए फिरते थे
दिल अजब कुंज-ए-अमाँ था पहले
अब भी तू पास नहीं है लेकिन
इस क़दर दूर कहाँ था पहले
डेरे डाले हैं बगूलों ने जहाँ
उस तरफ़ चश्मा रवाँ था पहले (8)
अब वो दरिया न वो बस्ती न वो लोग
क्या ख़बर कौन कहाँ था पहले   --continue--

47. Earlier too, a slight feel of waste I had

Earlier too, a slight feel of waste I had
But never in past the heart felt this bad

A little flutter and I get rattled now
Drunk I was earlier in a dreamy flow

Now the end of journey is moving on
Once my every step was a milestone

Never count the miles I ran in my quest
Time then was free from any arrest (4)

Though I'm at ease with heartache now
Yet it was a threat to life not long ago

Never in the past did I feel so restless
As heart was such a big source of solace

As always, you are not with me today
But were we ever so far apart this way?

Where we see a colony of herons now
There a waterfall once used to flow (8)

Now no sign of town, its people or river
Who knows who lived where once ever
      --Continue--

47. kuchh to ehsas-e-ziyan tha pahle

har kharaba ye sadaa deta hai
main bhi abaad makan tha pahle
ud gaye shakh se ye kah ke tuyyur
sarv ik shokh jawan tha pahle
kya se kya ho gayi duniya pyare
tu vahin par hai jahan tha pahle (12)
ham ne abaad kiya mulk-e-sukhan
kaisa sunsaan samaan tha pahle
ham ne bakhshi hai khamoshi ko zaban
dard majboor-e-fughan tha pahle
ham ne ijaad kiya tesha-e-ashk
shola patthar men nihan tha pahle
ham ne roshan kiya mamura-e-gham
varna har samt dhuaan tha pahle (16)
ham ne mahfooz kiya husn-e-bahar
itr-e-gul sarf-e-khizan tha pahle
gham ne phir dil ko jagaya 'nasir'
khana-barbad kahan tha pahle

हर ख़राबा ये सदा देता है
मैं भी आबाद मकाँ था पहले
उड़ गए शाख़ से ये कह के तुयूर
सर्व इक शोख़ जवाँ था पहले
क्या से क्या हो गई दुनिया प्यारे
तू वहीं पर है जहाँ था पहले (12)
हम ने आबाद किया मुल्क-ए-सुख़न
कैसा सुनसान समाँ था पहले
हम ने बख़्शी है ख़मोशी को ज़बाँ
दर्द मजबूर-ए-फ़ुगाँ था पहले
हम ने ईजाद किया तेशा-ए-अश्क
शो'ला पत्थर में निहाँ था पहले
हम ने रौशन किया मामूरा-ए-ग़म
वर्ना हर सम्त धुआँ था पहले (16)
हम ने महफ़ूज़ किया हुस्न-ए-बहार
इत्र-ए-गुल सर्फ़-ए-ख़िज़ाँ था पहले
ग़म ने फिर दिल को जगाया 'नासिर'
ख़ाना-बर्बाद कहाँ था पहले

47. Earlier too, a slight feel of waste I had

Every dump of ruins speaks in silence
I too was a home well-inhabited once

Birds flew away from the tree saying
It was once tall, young and glowing

The world has seen such a change, dear
But you stay exactly where you were (12)

We have revived the realm of poetry
How deserted earlier was this territory

We have bestowed speech to silence
Pain depended solely on crying once

We have introduced tears as pickaxe
Earlier fire remained buried in rocks

We have lighted the abode of sorrows
It was all wrapped up in smoke of woes (16)

We have preserved the beauty of spring
Fall used to devour the scent flowers bring

Grief brought the heart back to life 'Nasir'
Where in the dumps was it lying earlier

48. *kuchh yadgar-e-shahr-e-sitamgar hi le chalen*

*kuchh yadgar-e-shahr-e-sitamgar hi le chalen
aaye hain is gali men to patthar hi le chalen
yun kis tarah katega kadi dhoop ka safar
sar par khayal-e-yaar ki chadar hi le chalen
ranj-e-safar ki koyi nishani to paas ho
thodi si khak-e-kucha-e-dilbar hi le chalen
ye kah ke chhedti hai hamen dil-giraftagi
ghabra gaye hain aap to bahar hi le chalen (4)
is shahr-e-becharagh men jaayegi tu kahan
aa ai shab-e-firaq tujhe ghar hi le chalen*

कुछ यादगार-ए-शहर-ए-सितमगर ही ले चलें
आए हैं इस गली में तो पत्थर ही ले चलें
यूँ किस तरह कटेगा कड़ी धूप का सफ़र
सर पर ख़याल-ए-यार की चादर ही ले चलें
रंज-ए-सफ़र की कोई निशानी तो पास हो
थोड़ी सी ख़ाक-ए-कूचा-ए-दिलबर ही ले चलें
ये कह के छेड़ती है हमें दिल-गिरफ़्तगी
घबरा गये हैं आप तो बाहर ही ले चलें (4)
इस शहर-ए-बेचिराग़ में जाएगी तू कहाँ
आ ऐ शब-ए-फ़िराक़ तुझे घर ही ले चलें

48. Let us carry a souvenir from the city of the callous

Let us carry a souvenir from the city of the callous
Even a stray stone from its alley can be good for us

How can we undergo this journey in the blazing sun
A headcover of musings on the beloved may help us

Some tokens we must retain of this harsh journey
Let us carry a little dust from the lover's quarters

My self-confinement mocks at my heart saying
We can go out in the open, if you feel so nervous (4)

Where shall you go by yourself in this unlit town
Come on lonely night, you can head home with us

49. kya zamana tha ki ham roz mila karte the

kya zamana tha ki ham roz mila karte the
rat-bhar chand ke hamrah phira karte the
jahan tanhaiyan sar phod ke so jaati hain
in makanon men ajab log raha karte the
kar diya aaj zamane ne unhen bhi majboor
kabhi ye log mere dukh ki dava karte the
dekh kar jo hamen chupchap guzar jaata hai
kabhi us shakhs ko ham pyaar kiya karte the (4)
ittefaaqat-e-zamana bhi ajab hain 'nasir'
aaj vo dekh rahe hain jo suna karte the

क्या ज़माना था कि हम रोज़ मिला करते थे
रात भर चाँद के हमराह फिरा करते थे
जहाँ तनहाइयाँ सर फोड़ के सो जाती हैं
इन मकानों में अजब लोग रहा करते हैं
कर दिया आज ज़माने ने उन्हें भी मजबूर
कभी ये लोग मिरे दुख की दवा करते थे
देख कर जो हमें चुपचाप गुज़र जाता है
कभी उस शख़्स को हम प्यार किया करते थे (4)
इत्तिफ़ाक़ात-ए-ज़माना भी अजब है 'नासिर'
आज वो देख रहे हैं जो सुना करते थे

49. What good days were those when we met daily

What good days were those when we met daily
Alongside the moon, used to take a walk nightly

Where loneliness sleeps after an acute breakdown
In those houses, lived once people extraordinary

Times today have made even those folks helpless
Who, for all my troubles, were once a real therapy

Who now gives me a look and passes by in silence
Is the one who once upon a time, I loved dearly (4)

What serendipity, a quirky twist of fate, 'Nasir'
What was once only heard is now here to see

50. *kyun gham-e-raftagan kare koyi*

kyun gham-e-raftagan kare koyi
fikr-e-vamaandgan kare koyi
tere awaargan-e-ghurbat ko
shamil karvan kare koyi
zindagi ke azaab kya kam hain
kyun gham-e-lamakan kare koyi
dil tapakne laga hai ankhon se
ab kise razdan kare koyi(4)
us chaman men ba-rang-e-nikahat-e-gul
umr kyun raayegan kare koyi
shahr men shor ghar men tanhai
dil ki baaten kahan kare koyi
ye kharabe zaroor chamkenge
aitebar-e-khizan kare koyi

क्यूँ ग़म-ए-रफ़्तगाँ करे कोई
फ़िक्र-ए-वामाँदगाँ करे कोई
तेरे आवारगान-ए-ग़ुर्बत को
शामिल कारवाँ करे कोई
ज़िंदगी के अज़ाब क्या कम हैं
क्यूँ ग़म-ए-लामकाँ करे कोई
दिल टपकने लगा है आँखों से
अब किसे राज़दाँ करे कोई (4)
उस चमन में ब-रंग-ए-निकहत-ए-गुल
उम्र क्यूँ राएगाँ करे कोई
शहर में शोर घर में तन्हाई
दिल की बातें कहाँ करे कोई
ये ख़राबे ज़रूर चमकेंगे
ए'तिबार-ए-ख़िज़ाँ करे कोई

50. Why would one cry for those departed

Why would one cry for those departed
or care for those left behind exhausted

Those homeless left abandoned by exile
Will any caravan have them adopted?

As if there are fewer troubles in this life
Why add more of the other-life, uninvited

My heart is now dripping from my eyes
Can one still keep his feelings confided? (4)

Like flowers that let go their fragrance
Why waste your lifetime in that orchard

City has deafening din, home is lonely
Where can the heart share a talk candid

This wasteland will sparkle once again
Keep your faith till the autumn departed

51. mahroom-e-khwab dida-e-hairan na tha kabhi

mahroom-e-khwab dida-e-hairan na tha kabhi
tera ye rang ai shab-e-hijran na tha kabhi
tha lutf-e-vasl aur kabhi afsoon-e-intizar
yun dard-e-hijr silsila-jumban na tha kabhi
pursaan na tha koi to ye rusvaiyan na thi
zahir kisi pe hal-e-pareshan na tha kabhi
harchand gham bhi tha magar ehsas-e-gham na tha
darman na tha to matam-e-darman na tha kabhi (4)
din bhi udaas aur meri raat bhi udaas
aisa to waqt ai gham-e-dauran na tha kabhi
daur-e-khizaan men yun mere dil ko qaraar hai
main jaise aashna-e-bahaaran na tha kabhi
kya din the jab nazar men khizan bhi bahaar thi
yun apna ghar bahaar men viran na tha kabhi
be-kaif be-nishat na thi is qadar hayat
jeena agarche ishq men aasan na tha kabhi (8)

महरूम-ए-ख़्वाब दीदा-ए-हैराँ न था कभी
तेरा ये रंग ऐ शब-ए-हिज्राँ न था कभी
था लुत्फ़-ए-वस्ल और कभी अफ़्सून-ए-इंतिज़ार
यूँ दर्द-ए-हिज्र सिलसिला-जुम्बाँ न था कभी
पुरसाँ न था कोई तो ये रुस्वाइयाँ न थीं
ज़ाहिर किसी पे हाल-ए-परेशाँ न था कभी
हर-चंद ग़म भी था मगर एहसास-ए-ग़म न था
दरमाँ न था तो मातम-ए-दरमाँ न था कभी (4)
दिन भी उदास और मिरी रात भी उदास
ऐसा तो वक़्त ऐ ग़म-ए-दौराँ न था कभी
दौर-ए-ख़िज़ाँ में यूँ मेरे दिल को क़रार है
मैं जैसे आश्ना-ए-बहाराँ न था कभी
क्या दिन थे जब नज़र में ख़िज़ाँ भी बहार थी
यूँ अपना घर बहार में वीराँ न था कभी
बे-कैफ़ बे-नशात न थी इस क़दर हयात
जीना अगरचे इश्क़ में आसाँ न था कभी (8)

51. My curious eyes were never so bereft of dreams

My curious eyes were never so bereft of dreams
Nor was the lonely night ever so dull, it seems

There was pleasure in meeting, charm in waiting
This run of pain of parting was never so daunting

When no one cared, never had I any regrets
Nor did anybody realise how miserable it gets

Every minuite a pain it was, yet I could endure
As no antidote it had, never did I cry over cure

My days are wretched and so are the nights
Never before had I a bout of such painful bites

Autumn gives my heart such a great consolation
As if I had never known the spring's celebration

How good it was when I sensed spring in autumn
My home thus ceased to be barren in springtime

Life was never so dismal, unpleasant as it is now
Though it was never easy under the vows of love (8)

52. main hun raat ka ek baja hai

main hun raat ka ek baja hai
khali rasta bol raha hai
aaj to yun khamosh hai duniya
jaise kuchh hone vaala hai
kaisi andheri raat hai dekho
apne aap se dar lagta hai
aaj to shahr ki ravish ravish par
patton ka mela sa laga hai (4)
aao ghaas pe sabha jamaayen
maikhana to band pada hai
phool to saare jhad gaye lekin
teri yaad ka zakhm hara hai
tu ne jitna pyaar kiya tha
dukh bhi mujhe utna hi diya hai

मैं हूँ, रात का एक बजा है
ख़ाली रस्ता बोल रहा है
आज तो यूँ ख़ामोश है दुनिया
जैसे कुछ होने वाला है
कैसी अँधेरी रात है देखो
अपने आप से डर लगता है
आज तो शहर की रविश-रविश पर
पत्तों का मेला-सा लगा है (4)
आओ घास पे सभा जमायें
मैख़ाना तो बंद पड़ा है
फूल तो सारे झड़ गये लेकिन
तेरी याद का ज़ख़्म हरा है
तूने जितना प्यार किया था
दुख भी मुझे उतना ही दिया है
--continue-

52. It is me in the night one o'clock

It is me in the night one o'clock
Listening to the lonely road talk

The world is silent today, as if
It is up to some kind of mischief

Look, how densely dark it is tonight
One can get from himself a fright

Every street of the city has today
An exhibition of leaves on display (4)

Let us have party on a green patch
The bar today has a lock and latch

Flowers have dried and dropped
Alive in me is the lesion you caused

Much as I received love from you
Suffering in return was equal too
                          --continue--

52. main hun raat ka ek baja hai

ye bhi ek tarah ki mohabbat
main tujh se tu mujh se juda hai (8)
ye teri manzil vo mera rasta
tera mera saath hi kya hai
main ne to ik baat kahi thi
kya tu sachmuch ruth gaya hai
aisa gahak kaun hai jis ne
sukh de kar dukh mol liya hai
tera rasta takte takte
khet gagan ka sukh chala hai (12)
khidki khol ke dekh to bahar
der se koi shakhs khada hai
saari basti so gayi 'nasir'
tu ab tak kyun jaag raha hai

ये भी एक तरह की मोहब्बत
मैं तुझसे, तू मुझसे जुदा है (8)
ये तेरी मंज़िल, वो मेरा रस्ता
तेरा मेरा साथ ही क्या है
मैंने तो इक बात कही थी
क्या तू सचमुच रूठ गया है
ऐसा गाहक कौन है जिसने
सुख देकर दुख मोल लिया है
तेरा रस्ता तकते-तकते
खेत गगन का सूख चला है (12)
खिड़की खोल के देख तो बाहर
देर से कोई शख़्स खड़ा है
सारी बस्ती सो गई 'नासिर'
तू अब तक क्यों जाग रहा है

52. It is me in the night one o'clock

It is a love story of a different sort
I from you, you from me live apart (8)

This is your end and that is my way
What is common between us to say

I just said something, just as I did
Are you upset, or really offended

Who can be such a silly customer
Who would buy pain for pleasure

Looking ahead, waiting for you
Sky, like a field, turned dry in hue (12)

Open the window and out you look
A man for long is waiting in the nook

The town has gone to sleep 'Nasir'
Why are you still up at this hour

53. main is shahar men kyon aaya tha

main is shahar men kyon aaya tha
mera kaun yahan rahata tha
goonge ṭeelon, kuchh to bolo
kaun is nagari kaa raaja tha
kin logon ke hain ye ḍhaanche
kin maaon ne inko jana tha
kis devi ki hai ye moorat
kaun yahan pooja karata tha (4)
kis duniya ki kavita hai ye
kin haathon ne ise likha tha
kis gori ke hain ye kngan
ye kantha kisne pahana tha
kin waqton ke hain ye khilone
kaun yahan khela karata tha
bol meri mitti ki chidiya
tune mujh ko yaad kiya tha (8)

मैं इस शहर में क्यों आया था
मेरा कौन यहाँ रहता था
गूँगे टीलों, कुछ तो बोलो
कौन इस नगरी का राजा था
किन लोगों के हैं ये ढाँचे
किन माँओं ने इनको जना था
किस देवी की है ये मूरत
कौन यहाँ पूजा करता था (4)
किस दुनिया की कविता है ये
किन हाथों ने इसे लिखा था
किस गोरी के हैं ये कंगन
ये कण्ठा किसने पहना था
किन वक़्तों के हैं ये खिलौने
कौन यहाँ खेला करता था
बोल मिरी मिट्टी की चिड़िया
तूने मुझको याद किया था (8)

53. Why did I turn to this city

Why did I turn to this city
Was here anyone known to me

Mute mounts! Say something
Who was the king of this city

Which mothers raised them
Whose statues here we see

What goddess this idol is
And who were her devotee (4)

Whose hands wrote these
Which lands had this poetry

Which damsel had this bracelet
Whose necklace it used to be

Of what times these toys are
Who played with them in glee

Would you tell, my clay bird
Have you ever missed me (8)

54. *main ne jab likhna sikha tha*

main ne jab likhna sikha tha
pahle tera naam likha tha
main vo sabr-e-samim hun jis ne
baar-e-amanat sar pe liya tha
main vo ism-e-azeem hun jis ko
jinn-o-malak ne sajda kiya tha
tu ne kyun mera haath na pakda
main jab raste se bhatka tha (4)
jo paaya hai vo tera hai
jo khoya vo bhi tera tha
tujh bin saari umr guzari
log kahenge tu mera tha
pahli barish bhejne vaale
main tere darshan ka pyasa tha
tire dhyaan ki kashti lekar
main ne dariya paar kiya tha (8)
tere ghar ke darwaaze par
suraj nange paanv khada tha

मैंने जब लिखना सीखा था
पहले तेरा नाम लिखा था
मैं वो सब्र-ए-समीम हूँ जिस ने
बार-ए-अमानत सर पे लिया था
मैं वो इस्म-ए-अज़ीम हूँ जिस को
जिन्न-ओ-मलक ने सज्दा किया था
तूने क्यों मिरा हाथ न पकड़ा
मैं जब रस्ते से भटका था (4)
जो पाया है वो तेरा है
जो खोया वो भी तेरा था
तुझ बिन सारी उम्र गुज़ारी
लोग कहेंगे तू मेरा था
पहली बारिश भेजने वाले
मैं तिरे दर्शन का प्यासा था
तेरे ध्यान की कश्ती लेकर
मैंने दरिया पार किया था (8)
तेरे घर के दरवाज़े पर
सूरज नंगे पाँव खड़ा था

54. When I learnt the writing code

When I learnt the writing code
First of all, your name I wrote

I am that sincere, patient one*
Who accepted the divine load

I bear the noble name to whom**
The djinns and angels bowed

Why didn't you hold me back
When I went off the road (4)

What I gained was all yours
What I lost was all you bestowed

All my life I lived without you
They say you lived in my abode

You, who sent the first rains
A meeting with you I implored

I crossed the river on a mind-boat
With you in my thought on board (8)

The Sun standing barefoot
Was waiting at your threshold

*Reference to The Quran where Man took the burden of the universe and acquired the power of direct communion with God.
** Reference to when angels were ordained to bow to Adam before he left the Paradise for earth.

55. *mujh ko aur kahin jaana tha*

mujh ko aur kahin jaana tha
bas yunhi rasta bhool gaya tha
dekh ke tere des ki rachna
main ne safar mauquf kiya tha
kaisi andheri shaam thi us din
badal bhi ghir kar chhaya tha
raat ki toofani barish men
tu mujh se milne aaya tha (4)
mathe par boondon ke moti
ankhon men kajal hansta tha
chandi ka ik phool gale men
haath men badal ka tukda tha

मुझ को और कहीं जाना था
बस यूँही रस्ता भूल गया था
देख के तेरे देस की रचना
मैं ने सफ़र मौकूफ़ किया था
कैसी अँधेरी शाम थी उस दिन
बादल भी घिर कर आया था
रात की तूफ़ानी बारिश में
तू मुझ से मिलने आया था (4)
माथे पर बूंदों के मोती
आँखों में काजल हँसता था
चाँदी का इक फूल गले में
हाथ में बादल का टुकड़ा था
--Continue--

55. I had to go another direction

I had to go another direction
But lost my way for no reason

After witnessing your environs
I postponed my expedition

How dark that evening was
Hordes of cloud did overrun

In torrential rain that night
You came to meet for a union (4)

On your brow drops of pearls
In your eyes kohl having fun

Around your neck a silver locket
In your hands a cloud in a bun
                    --continue--

55. mujh ko aur kahin jaana tha

bheege kapde ki lahron men
kundan sona damak raha tha
sabz pahadi ke daaman men
us din kitna hangama tha (8)
baarish ki tirchhi galiyon men
koyi charagh liye phirta tha
bheegi bheegi khamoshi men
main tere ghar tak saath gaya tha
ek taveel safar ka jhonka
mujh ko door liye jaata tha

भीगे कपड़े की लहरों में
कुंदन सोना दमक रहा था
सब्ज़ पहाड़ी के दामन में
उस दिन कितना हंगामा था (8)
बारिश की तिरछी गलियों में
कोई चराग़ लिए फिरता था
भीगी भीगी ख़ामोशी में
मैं तिरे घर तक साथ गया था
एक तवील सफ़र का झोंका
मुझ को दूर लिए जाता था

55. I had to go another direction

In your breezy soaked dress
Glowed the form pure golden

Near the green hill that day
Did you see a huge commotion? (8)

In the slanted rainy streets
Someone walked with a lantern

In the wet soggy silence, a walk
To drop you home I had taken

An outspread journey on wind
Pushed me far on a long run

56. *mumkin nahin mata-e-sukhan mujh se chheen le*

mumkin nahin mata-e-sukhan mujh se chheen le
go baghban ye kunj-e-chaman mujh se chheen le
gar ehtiram-e-rasm-e-wafa hai to ai khuda
ye ehtiram-e-rasm-e-kohan mujh se chheen le
manzar dil o nigah ke jab ho gaye udaas
ye be-faza ilaqa-e-tan mujh se chheen le
gulrez meri nala-kashi se hai shaakh shaakh
gulchin ka bas chale to ye fan mujh se chheen le (4)
sinchi hain dil ke khoon se maine ye kiyariyan
kis ki majal mera chaman mujh se chheen le

मुमकिन नहीं मता-ए-सुख़न मुझ से छीन ले
गो बाग़बाँ ये कुंज-ए-चमन मुझ से छीन ले
गर एहतिराम-ए-रस्म-ए-वफ़ा है तो ऐ ख़ुदा
ये एहतिराम-ए-रस्म-ए-कोहन मुझ से छीन ले
मंज़र दिल ओ निगाह के जब हो गए उदास
ये बे-फ़ज़ा इलाक़ा-ए-तन मुझ से छीन ले
गुल-रेज़ मेरी नाला-कशी से है शाख़ शाख़
गुलचीं का बस चले तो ये फ़न मुझ से छीन ले (4)
सींची हैं दिल के ख़ून से मैं ने ये कियारियाँ
किस की मजाल मेरा चमन मुझ से छीन ले

56. No way can he take away my power to articulate

No way can he take away my power to articulate
Though gardener can throw me out of his estate

If there is some honour in following a tradition
Then O God! Free me from this old convention

When eye and heart see only a sad spectacle
Wrest from me this airy terrain of body feeble

With my cries, I make every bough cast flowers
Left to the florist, he will strip me of my powers (4)

With my heart and blood, I have nursed this yard
How can I let anyone snatch away my orchard?

57. *musalsal bekali dil ko rahi hai*

musalsal bekali dil ko rahi hai
magar jeene ki surat to rahi hai
main kyun phirta hun tanha maara maara
ye basti chain se kyun so rahi hai
chale dil se umeedon ke musafir
ye nagri aaj khali ho rahi hai
na samjho tum ise shor-e-bahaaran
khizan patton men chhup kar ro rahi hai (4)
hamare ghar ki deewaron pe 'nasir'
udasi baal khole so rahi hai

मुसलसल बेकली दिल को रही है
मगर जीने की सूरत तो रही है
मैं क्यों फिरता हूँ तनहा, मारा-मारा
ये बस्ती चैन से क्यों सो रही है
चले दिल से उम्मीदों के मुसाफ़िर
ये नगरी आज ख़ाली हो रही है
न समझो तुम इसे शोर-ए-बहाराँ
ख़िज़ाँ पत्तों में छुप कर रो रही है (4)
हमारे घर की दीवारों पे 'नासिर'
उदासी बाल खोले सो रही है

57. Heart had its restlessness all the time

Heart had its restlessness all the time
Yet had reasons to live on all the time

Why do I meander alone and wretchedly
When neighbours sleep like peacetime

Hope is now drifting away from the heart
This city is being evacuated for the time

Don't you misread the springtime revel
It is autumn crying behind the leafy chime (4)

On the walls of our home 'Nasir', gloom
With its hair down is sleeping like bedtime

58. *naye kapde badal kar jaun kahan*

naye kapde badal kar jaun kahan aur baal banaun kis ke liye
vo shakhs to shahr hi chhod gaya main bahar jaun kis ke liye
jis dhup ki dil men thandak thi vo dhup usi ke saath gayi
in jalti bujhati galiyon men ab khaak udaun kis ke liye
vo shahr men tha to us ke liye auron se bhi milna padta tha
ab aise-vaise logon ke main naaz uthaun kis ke liye
ab shahr men us ka badal hi nahin koyi vaisa jaan-e-ghazal hi nahin
aivaan-e-ghazal men lafzon ke guldaan sajaun kis ke liye (4)
muddat se koyi aaya na gaya sunsan padi hai ghar ki faza
in khali kamron men 'nasir' ab shama jalaun kis ke liye

नये कपड़े बदलकर जाऊँ कहाँ और बाल बनाऊँ किसके लिए
वो शख़्स तो शहर ही छोड़ गया, मैं बाहर जाऊँ किसके लिए
जिस धूप की दिल में ठण्डक थी वो धूप उसी के साथ गयी
इन जलती-बुझती गलियों में अब ख़ाक उड़ाऊँ किसके लिए
वो शहर में था तो उसके लिए औरों से भी मिलना पड़ता था
अब ऐसे-वैसे लोगों के मैं नाज़ उठाऊँ किसके लिए
अब शहर में उसका बदल ही नहीं, कोई वैसा जान-ए-ग़ज़ल ही नहीं
ऐवान-ए-ग़ज़ल में लफ़्ज़ों के गुलदान सजाऊँ किसके लिए (4)
मुद्दत से कोई आया न गया सुनसान पड़ी है घर की फ़ज़ा
इन ख़ाली कमरों में 'नासिर' अब शम्अ जलाऊँ किसके लिए

58. Who should I get dressed up for

Who should I get dressed up for and have my hair blown
For the one I used to go out with has already left the town

The sunshine that kept my heart cool has vanished with him
Why should then I trudge these streets, half-lighted and dim

Whenever in town with him, I had to mingle with others
Why should I care now for all those who nobody bothers

The town has no one to replace him, none as much literary
Who should then I present my bouquet of words in poetry (4)

For long no one has come or gone, deserted lies the home
Why should then 'Nasir' light up these rooms and for whom

59. *nasib-e-ishq dil-e-beqaraar bhi to nahin*

nasib-e-ishq dil-e-beqaraar bhi to nahin
bahut dinon se tera intizaar bhi to nahin
talafi-e-sitam-e-rozgaar kaun kare
tu hamsukhan bhi nahin razdaar bhi to nahin
zamana pursish-e-gham bhi kare to kya hasil
ki tera gham gham-e-lail-o-nihaar bhi to nahin
teri nigah-e-taghaful ko kaun samjhaaye
ki apne dil pe mujhe ikhtiyaar bhi to nahin (4)
tu hi bata ki teri khamoshi ko kya samjhun
teri nigah se kuchh aashkaar bhi to nahin
wafa nahin na sahi rasm-o-rah kya kam hai
teri nazar ka magar aitibaar bhi to nahin

नसीब-ए-इश्क़ दिल-ए-बे-क़रार भी तो नहीं
बहुत दिनों से तिरा इंतिज़ार भी तो नहीं
तलाफ़ी-ए-सितम-ए-रोज़गार कौन करे
तू हम-सुखन भी नहीं राज़-दार भी तो नहीं
ज़माना पुर्सिश-ए-ग़म भी करे तो क्या हासिल
कि तेरा ग़म ग़म-ए-लैल-ओ-निहार भी तो नहीं
तिरी निगाह-ए-तग़ाफुल को कौन समझाए
कि अपने दिल पे मुझे इख़्तियार भी तो नहीं (4)
तू ही बता कि तिरी ख़ामुशी को क्या समझूँ
तिरी निगाह से कुछ आश्कार भी तो नहीं
वफ़ा नहीं न सही रस्म-ओ-राह क्या कम है
तिरी नज़र का मगर ए'तिबार भी तो नहीं

--continue--

59. Neither the bliss of love, nor a restless heart

Neither the bliss of love, nor a restless heart
For long no urge to meet you either on my part

Who can allay the daily run of our fears and fret
Not you, who don't share my tongue or my secret

What gain, if the world comes to nurse my grief
The pain you gave is no ordinary ordeal, in brief

How does one convey to your look of unconcern
That the pangs in my heart are hard to govern (4)

Only you can tell what to make of your silence
When your blank eyes simply leave no evidence

Forget sincerity, enough to have some courtesy
For how little do I trust even the way you see
                              --continue--

59. nasib-e-ishq dil-e-beqaraar bhi to nahin

agarche dil teri manzil na ban saka ai dost
magar charagh-e-sar-e-rahguzaar bhi to nahin
bahut fasurda hai dil kaun is ko bahlaaye
udaas bhi to nahin beqaraar bhi to nahin (8)
tu hi bata tere be-khanuman kidhar jaayen
ki raah men shajar sayadaar bhi to nahin
falak ne phenk diya barg-e-gul ki chhanv se door
vahan pade hain jahan kharzaar bhi to nahin
jo zindagi hai to bas tere dard-mandon ki
ye jabr bhi to nahin ikhtiyaar bhi to nahin
wafa zariya-e-izhaar-e-gham sahi 'nasir'
ye karobaar koyi karobaar bhi to nahin (12)

अगरचे दिल तिरी मंज़िल न बन सका ऐ दोस्त
मगर चराग़-ए-सर-ए-रहगुज़ार भी तो नहीं
बहुत फ़सुर्दा है दिल कौन इस को बहलाए
उदास भी तो नहीं बे-क़रार भी तो नहीं (8)
तू ही बता तिरे बे-ख़ानुमाँ किधर जाएँ
कि राह में शजर साया-दार भी तो नहीं
फ़लक ने फेंक दिया बर्ग-ए-गुल की छाँव से दूर
वहाँ पड़े हैं जहाँ ख़ार-ज़ार भी तो नहीं
जो ज़िंदगी है तो बस तेरे दर्द-मंदों की
ये जब्र भी तो नहीं इख़्तियार भी तो नहीं
वफ़ा ज़रीया-ए-इज़हार-ए-ग़म सही 'नासिर'
ये कारोबार कोई कारोबार भी तो नहीं (12)

59. Neither the bliss of love, nor a restless heart

The heart not only did not end up as your guide
It even failed to provide any light on the wayside

Who can cheer up this heart, aggrieved as it is
When not much depressed nor annoyed it is (8)

Tell me where they can go the ones you forsake
On the way there are not even trees with shade

Heaven has hurled us away from flower portals
Where we have now not even a bed of nettles

Life goes well with those who come in your fold
Otherwise, it is neither oppressed nor in control

Loyalty surely is a contract to share woes 'Nasir'
But such a contract is not exactly a trade either (12)

60. 'nasir' kya kahta phirta hai

'nasir' kya kahta phirta hai kuchh na suno to behtar hai
deewana hai deewane ke munh na lago to behtar hai
kal jo tha vo aaj nahin jo aaj hai kal mit jayega
rukhi-sukhi jo mil jaaye shukr karo to behtar hai
kal ye taab-o-tawan na rahegi thanda ho jayega lahu
naam-e-khuda ho jawaan abhi kuchh kar guzro to behtar hai
kya jaane kya rut badle halaat ka koyi theek nahin
ab ke safar men tum bhi hamare saath chalo to behtar hai (4)
kapde badal kar baal bana kar kahan chale ho kis ke liye
raat bahut kaali hai 'nasir' ghar men raho to behtar hai

'नासिर' क्या कहता फिरता है, कुछ न सुनो तो बेहतर है
दीवाना है दीवाने के मुँह न लगो तो बेहतर है
कल जो था वो आज नहीं, जो आज है कल मिट जाएगा
रूखी-सूखी जो मिल जाए, शुक्र करो तो बेहतर है
कल ये ताब-ओ-तवाँ न रहेगी ठण्डा हो जाएगा लहू
नाम-ए-खुदा हो जवान अभी कुछ कर गुज़रो तो बेहतर है
क्या जाने क्या रुत बदले, हालात का कोई ठीक नहीं
अब के सफ़र में तुम भी हमारे साथ चलो तो बेहतर है (4)
कपड़े बदलकर, बाल बनाकर कहाँ चले हो, किसके लिए
रात बहुत काली है 'नासिर' घर में रहो तो बेहतर है

60. Whatever 'Nasir' says

Whatever 'Nasir' says, if you listen not, it is better
He is crazy; if you don't argue with him, it is better

What we had didn't last, what we have will go too
Enjoy with gratitude the little you get, it is better

Tomorrow blood will not be warm, vigour may fail
For God's sake, make the best of youth, it is better

Who can tell when seasons and scenes may alter
 If you join us on the mission this time, it is better (4)

Where do you go, all dressed up and well groomed
Pitch dark is the night 'Nasir', stay home, it is better

61. *naaz-e-begaanagi men kya kuchh tha*

naaz-e-begaanagi men kya kuchh tha
husn ki saadgi men kya kuchh tha
laakh rahen theen laakh jalwe the
ahd-e-awaargi men kya kuchh tha
aankh khulte hi chhup gayi har shai
aalam-e-bekhudi men kya kuchh tha
yaad hain marhale mohabbat ke
haaye us bekali men kya kuchh tha (4)
kitne beete dinon ki yaad aai
aaj teri kami men kya kuchh tha
kitne manus log yaad aaye
subah ki chandni men kya kuchh tha
raat bhar ham na so sake 'nasir'
parda-e-khamoshi men kya kuchh tha

नाज़-ए-बेगानगी में क्या कुछ था
हुस्न की सादगी में क्या कुछ था
लाख राहें थीं, लाख जलवे थे
अहद-ए-आवारगी में क्या कुछ था
आँख खुलते ही छुप गई हर शै
आलम-ए-बेख़ुदी में क्या कुछ था
याद हैं मरहले मुहब्बत के
हाय उस बेकली में क्या कुछ था (4)
कितने बीते दिनों की याद आई
आज तेरी कमी में क्या कुछ था
कितने मानूस लोग याद आए
सुब्ह की चाँदनी में क्या कुछ था
रात-भर हम न सो सके 'नासिर'
परदा-ए-ख़ामुशी में क्या कुछ था

61. Her conceited unconcern had a lot in it

Her conceited unconcern had a lot in it
Beauty in simplicity too had a lot in it

Many trails to follow, many marvels to see
The time of free-wheeling had a lot in it

When eyes opened everything vanished
The state of blind amnesia had a lot in it

I can recall many ups and downs of love
Ah! that state of unrest had a lot in it (4)

Memories of the past came storming
Today, I felt your absence had a lot in it

How many old familiar faces came alive
Early morning moonlight had a lot in it

I could not sleep the whole night 'Nasir'
The dark cover of silence had a lot in it

62. niyyat-e-shauq bhar na jaye kahin

niyyat-e-shauq bhar na jaye kahin
tu bhi dil se utar na jaye kahin
aaj dekha hai tujh ko der ke baad
aaj ka din guzar na jaye kahin
na mila kar udaas logon se
husn tera bikhar na jaye kahin
aarzu hai ki tu yahan aaye
aur phir umr bhar na jaye kahin (4)
ji jalata hun aur sochta hun
rayegan ye hunar na jaye kahin
aao kuchh der ro hi len 'nasir'
phir ye dariya utar na jaye kahin

नीयत-ए-शौक़ भर न जाए कहीं
तू भी दिल से उतर न जाए कहीं
आज देखा है तुझको देर के बाद
आज का दिन गुज़र न जाए कहीं
न मिला कर उदास लोगों से
हुस्न तेरा बिखर न जाए कहीं
आरज़ू है कि तू यहाँ आए
और फिर उम्र भर न जाए कहीं (4)
जी जलाता हूँ और सोचता हूँ
रायगाँ ये हुनर न जाए कहीं
आज कुछ देर रो ही लें 'नासिर'
फिर ये दरिया उतर न जाए कहीं

62. What if love gets full and fades away

What if love gets full and fades away
What if the heart too casts you away

Today I see you after a long time
I hope the day doesn't soon pass away

Don't you ever meet those in sorrow
You may have your charm blown away

I wish you decide to come back
And then choose never to go away (4)

I burn up within and contemplate
This art I may not just fritter away

Let me shed a few more tears 'Nasir'
This river in spate may soon ebb away

63. *o mere masroof khuda*

o mere masroof khuda
apni duniya dekh zara
itni khalqat ke hote
shahron men hai sannata
jhonpadi valon ki taqdeer
bujha bujha sa ek diya
khaak udaate hain din raat
meelon phail gaye sahra (4)
suraj sar pe aa pahuncha
garmi hai ya roz-e-jaza
pyaasi dharti jalti hai
sookh gaye bahte dariya
faslen jal kar raakh huyeen
nagri nagri kaal pada

ओ मेरे मसरूफ़ ख़ुदा
अपनी दुनिया देख ज़रा
इतनी ख़ल्क़त के होते
शहरों में है सन्नाटा
झोंपड़ी वालों की तक़दीर
बुझा-बुझा-सा एक दिया
ख़ाक उड़ाते हैं दिन-रात
मीलों फैल गये सहरा (4)
सूरज सर पर आ पहुँचा
गर्मी है या रोज़-ए-जज़ा
प्यासी धरती जलती है
सूख गये बहते दरिया
फ़सलें जलकर राख हुईं
नगरी-नगरी काल पड़ा

63. Oh, My busy busy Lord!

Oh, My busy busy Lord!
See the world and its state

Despite being so crowded
Cities are dark and desolate

Slum dwellers and their fate
The dim light is about to fade

The dust is rising day and night
For miles deserts permeate (4)

The noon sun is high on us
Is it heat or a fire to decimate?

The scorched earth is burning
No water in rivers to irrigate

The crops have turned into ash
Not a grain on anyone's plate

64. *parde men har awaaz ke shamil to vahi hai*

*parde men har awaaz ke shamil to vahi hai
ham laakh badal jaayen magar dil to vahi hai
mauzu-e-sukhan hai vahi afsana-e-shirin
mahfil ho koi raunaq-e-mahfil to vahi hai
mahsoos jo hota hai dikhai nahin deta
dil aur nazar men had-e-faazil to vahi hai
har chand tere lutf se mahroom nahin ham
lekin dil-e-betab ki mushkil to vahi hai (4)
girdab se nikle bhi to jayenge kahan ham
doobi thi jahan naav ye sahil to vahi hai
lut jaate hain din ko bhi jahan qaafile vaale
hushiyar musafir ki ye manzil to vahi hai
vo rang vo awaaz vo saj aur vo surat
sach kahte ho tum pyaar ke qaabil to vahi hai
sad-shukr ki is haal men jeete to hain 'nasir'
hasil na sahi kaavish-e-hasil to vahi hai (8)*

पर्दे में हर आवाज़ के शामिल तो वही है
हम लाख बदल जाएँ मगर दिल तो वही है
मौज़ू-ए-सुख़न है वही अफ़साना-ए-शीरीं
महफ़िल हो कोई रौनक़-ए-महफ़िल तो वही है
महसूस जो होता है दिखाई नहीं देता
दिल और नज़र में हद-ए-फ़ाज़िल तो वही है
हर चंद तिरे लुत्फ़ से महरूम नहीं हम
लेकिन दिल-ए-बेताब की मुश्किल तो वही है (4)
गिर्दाब से निकले भी तो जाएँगे कहाँ हम
डूबी थी जहाँ नाव ये साहिल तो वही है
लुट जाते हैं दिन को भी जहाँ क़ाफ़िले वाले
हुशियार मुसाफ़िर कि ये मंज़िल तो वही है
वो रंग वो आवाज़ वो सज और वो सूरत
सच कहते हो तुम प्यार के क़ाबिल तो वही है
सद-शुक्र कि इस हाल में जीते तो हैं 'नासिर'
हासिल न सही काविश-ए-हासिल तो वही है (8)

64. The one hidden in every voice is the same

The one hidden in every voice is the same
Much as we change, heart remains the same

The same sweet tale is the theme of all poetry
What brings life to every gathering is the same

What is felt is not always what can be seen
The gap between heart and eye is the same

Of course, we are never deprived of your bounty
Yet, the toil of the restless heart is the same (4)

Where can we go even if we cross the whirlpool
The shore where we lose our boat is the same

The place where caravans are robbed in daytime
And the alert voyagers wish to reach is the same

That gaiety, that voice, that dazzle, that visage
Right you are, the one worthy of love is the same

Thousand thanks 'Nasir', we are alive as we are
Even if no gains, the quest remains the same (8)

65. *patthar ka vo shahr bhi kya tha*

patthar ka vo shahr bhi kya tha
shahr ke niche shahr basa tha
ped bhi patthar phool bhi patthar
patta patta patthar ka tha
chand bhi patthar jheel bhi patthar
paani bhi patthar lagta tha
log bhi saare patthar ke the
rang bhi un ka patthar sa tha (4)
patthar ka ik saamp sunehra
kaale patthar se lipta tha
patthar ki andhi galiyon men
main tujhe saath liye phirta tha
goongi vaadi goonj uthti thi
jab koi patthar girta tha

पत्थर का वो शहर भी क्या था
शहर के नीचे शहर बसा था
पेड़ भी पत्थर फूल भी पत्थर
पत्ता पत्ता पत्थर का था
चाँद भी पत्थर झील भी पत्थर
पानी भी पत्थर लगता था
लोग भी सारे पत्थर के थे
रंग भी उन का पत्थर सा था (4)
पत्थर का इक साँप सुनहरा
काले पत्थर से लिपटा था
पत्थर की अंधी गलियों में
मैं तुझे साथ लिए फिरता था
गूँगी वादी गूँज उठती थी
जब कोई पत्थर गिरता था

65. All of stone it was, what a city

All of stone it was, what a city
Underneath it, was another city

The trees, the flowers were stones
Even the leaves were crusty

Moon looked a pebble, lake a rock
The water surface hard and frosty

Even People looked like statues
Their colour too had turned dusty (4)

Coiled around a dark stone
A golden snake was sitting pretty

In those dark cobblestone alleys
I took you to walk alongside me

The dumb valley would resound
At the fall of every rocky entity

66. *phool khushboo se juda hai ab ke*

phool khushboo se juda hai ab ke
yaaro ye kaisi hava hai ab ke
dost bichhde hain kai baar magar
ye naya daagh khila hai ab ke
pattiyan roti hain sar peetti hain
qatl-e-gul aam hua hai ab ke
shafqi ho gayi deewar-e-khayal
kis qadar khoon baha hai ab ke (4)
manzar-e-zakhm-e-wafa kis ko dikhayen
shahr men qaht-e-wafa hai ab ke
vo to phir ghair the lekin yaaro
kaam apnon se pada hai ab ke
kya sunen shor-e-bahaaran 'nasir'
ham ne kuchh aur suna hai ab ke

फूल ख़ुशबू से जुदा है अब के
यारों ये कैसी हवा है अब के
दोस्त बिछुड़े हैं कई बार मगर
ये नया दाग़ खिला है अब के
पत्तियाँ रोती हैं सर पीटती हैं
क़त्ल-ए-गुल आम हुआ अब के
शफ़क़ी हो गई दीवार-ए-ख़याल
किस क़दर ख़ून बहा है अब के (4)
मंज़र-ए-ज़ख़्म-ए-वफ़ा किसको दिखाएँ
शहर में क़हत-ए-वफ़ा है अब के
वो तो फिर ग़ैर थे लेकिन यारों
काम अपनों से पड़ा है अब के
क्या सुनें शोर-ए-बहाराँ 'नासिर'
हमने कुछ और सुना है अब के

66. Fragrance leaves the flowers this time

Fragrance leaves the flowers this time
What gusty winds, we have this time

We have lost friends earlier too, but
What a different scar it has left this time

Petals are wailing, breaking their heads
What a slaughter of flowers it is this time

Even the wall of my muse turned red
What a bloodshed we had this time (4)

Where do I exhibit my bruised faith
What a famine of trust in town this time

Yes, they were other than us that time
But, mates, they are our own this time

How can I relish the call of spring 'Nasir'
What I hear is something else this time

67. *qahr se dekh na har aan mujhe*

qahr se dekh na har aan mujhe
aankh rakhta hai to pehchaan mujhe
yak ba yak aake dikha do jhamaki
kyon firaate ho pareshaan mujhe
ek se ek nayi manzil men
liye firata hai tera dhyaan mujhe
sun ke awaaz-e-gul kuchh na suna
bas usee din se huye kaan mujhe (4)
jee thikane nahin jab se 'nasir'
shahr lagata hai bayabaan mujhe

क़हर से देख न हर आन मुझे
आँख रखता है तो पहचान मुझे
यकबयक आके दिखा दो झमकी
क्यों फिराते हो परेशान मुझे
एक से एक नयी मंज़िल में
लिए फिरता है तिरा ध्यान मुझे
सुन के आवाज़-ए-गुल कुछ न सुना
बस उसी दिन से हुए कान मुझे (4)
जी ठिकाने नहीं जब से 'नासिर'
शहर लगता है बयाबान मुझे

67. Don't you with stern eyes look at me

Don't you with stern eyes look at me
Make out who I am if you can see

Give me a glimpse, one and quick
Why torment me and make me sick

My mind immersed in your thought
Keeps drifting me to every new port

indeed, I received the alert the day
I didn't listen to what the flowers say (4)

Since then 'Nasir' has not been steady
The city seems nothing but all empty

68. *rah-e-junoon men khirad ka hawaala kya karta*

rah-e-junoon men khirad ka hawaala kya karta
ye khizr ranj-e-safar ka izaala kya karta
guzaarni thi tere hijr ki pahaad si raat
main tar-e-resham-o-zar ka doshaala kya karta
na shaghl-e-khara-tarashi na karobaar-e-junoon
main koh-o-dasht men faryad-o-naala kya karta
hikayat-e-gham-e-duniya ko chahiye daftar
varaq varaq mere dil ka risaala kya karta (4)
main trishna kaam tere maikade se laut aaya
kisi ke naam ka le kar pyaala kya karta

रह-ए-जुनूँ में ख़िरद का हवाला क्या करता
ये ख़िज़्र रंज-ए-सफ़र का इज़ाला क्या करता
गुज़ारनी थी तिरे हिज्र की पहाड़ सी रात
मैं तार-ए-रेशम-ओ-ज़र का दो-शाला क्या करता
न शग़्ल-ए-ख़ारा-तराशी न कारोबार-ए-जुनूँ
मैं कोह-ओ-दश्त में फ़र्याद-ओ-नाला क्या करता
हिकायत-ए-ग़म-ए-दुनिया को चाहिए दफ़्तर
वरक़ वरक़ मिरे दिल का रिसाला क्या करता (4)
मैं तिश्ना काम तिरे मय-कदे से लौट आया
किसी के नाम का ले कर प्याला क्या करता

68. Why talk of reason in the state of obsession

Why talk of reason in the state of obsession
What could Khizr* do for the on-road frustration

I had to spend that cold night of separation
What could a gold-silk shawl do for protection

When I am neither in mad love nor rock-felling**
Then why on a mountain shall I pray by yelling

The story of the worldly woes needs a full office
A few pages of my heart's journal won't suffice (4)

I came out thirsting for a drink from your tavern
How could I take a cup meant for another person

*refers to Saint Khizr, who guides people on the righteous path
**refers to Farhad, who was asked to dig a canal in a rocky mountain

69. rah-navard-e-bayabaan-e-gham sabr kar

rah-navard-e-bayabaan-e-gham sabr kar sabr kar
kaarvan phir milenge baham sabr kar sabr kar
be-nishaan hai safar raat saari padi hai magar
aa rahi hai sada dam-ba-dam sabr kar sabr kar
teri fariyad gunjegi dharti se akaash tak
koi din aur seh le sitam sabr kar sabr kar
tere qadmon se jagenge ujde dilon ke khutan
pa-shikasta ghazaal-e-haram sabr kar sabr kar (4)
shahr ujde to kya hai kushaada zamin-e-khuda
ik naya ghar banayenge ham sabr kar sabr kar
ye mahallat-e-shahi tabaahi ke hain muntazir
girne vaale hain un ke alam sabr kar sabr kar

रह-नवर्द-ए-बयाबान-ए-ग़म सब्र कर सब्र कर
कारवाँ फिर मिलेंगे बहम सब्र कर सब्र कर
बे-निशाँ है सफ़र रात सारी पड़ी है मगर
आ रही है सदा दम-ब-दम सब्र कर सब्र कर
तेरी फ़रियाद गूँजेगी धरती से आकाश तक
कोई दिन और सह ले सितम सब्र कर सब्र कर
तेरे क़दमों से जागेंगे उजड़े दिलों के ख़ुतन
पा-शिकस्ता ग़ज़ाल-ए-हरम सब्र कर सब्र कर (4)
शहर उजड़े तो क्या है कुशादा ज़मीन-ए-ख़ुदा
इक नया घर बनाएँगे हम सब्र कर सब्र कर
ये महल्लात-ए-शाही तबाही के हैं मुंतज़िर
गिरने वाले हैं उन के अलम सब्र कर सब्र कर

--continue--

69. Swirling in the wilderness of woes, keep patience

Swirling in the wilderness of woes, keep patience
Those caravans will come along, keep patience

The journey is wayward and a long night ahead
But there are voices every minute, keep patience

Your prayers will resound from the earth to sky
Brave this torture a few more days, keep patience

With your steps, musk will arise in ravaged hearts
O fatigued gazelle* of holy Mecca! Keep patience (4)

Cities are wrecked, yet there's land of God's plenty
We'll make another, a new home, keep patience

These royal palaces are waiting to be demolished
We will see their flags go down, keep patience
                                        --continue--

*legendary deer in the vicinity of Mecca who was saved by the Holy Prophet

69. rah-navard-e-bayabaan-e-gham sabr kar

daf bajayenge barg-o-shajar saf-ba-saf har taraf
khushk mitti se phutega nam sabr kar sabr kar
lahlahayengi phir khetiyan kaarvan kaarvan
khul ke barsega abr-e-karam sabr kar sabr kar (8)
kyun patakta hai sar sang se ji jala dhang se
dil hi ban jayega khud sanam sabr kar sabr kar
pahle khil jaaye dil ka kanwal phir likhenge ghazal
koi dam ai sarir-e-qalam sabr kar sabr kar
dard ke taar milne to de hont hilne to de
saari baten karenge raqam sabr kar sabr kar
dekh 'nasir' zamaane men koi kisi ka nahin
bhool ja us ke qaul-o-qasam sabr kar sabr kar (12)

डफ़ बजाएँगे बर्ग ओ शजर सफ़-ब-सफ़ हर तरफ़
ख़ुश्क मिट्टी से फूटेगा नम सब्र कर सब्र कर
लहलहाएँगी फिर खेतियाँ कारवाँ कारवाँ
खुल के बरसेगा अब्र-ए-करम सब्र कर सब्र कर (8)
क्यूँ पटकता है सर संग से जी जला ढंग से
दिल ही बन जाएगा ख़ुद सनम सब्र कर सब्र कर
पहले खिल जाए दिल का कँवल फिर लिखेंगे ग़ज़ल
कोई दम ऐ सरीर-ए-क़लम सब्र कर सब्र कर
दर्द के तार मिलने तो दे होंट हिलने तो दे
सारी बातें करेंगे रक़म सब्र कर सब्र कर
देख 'नासिर' ज़माने में कोई किसी का नहीं
भूल जा उस के क़ौल ओ क़सम सब्र कर सब्र कर (12)

69. Swirling in the wilderness of woes, keep patience

Row after row, trees and leaves will play the drum
From the dry land will spring water, keep patience

Along every settlement there will be a lush crop
Clouds of mercy will pour heavily, keep patience (8)

Why hit head on a stone, chisel your heart well
It will turn into an idol itself, keep patience

I will write a ghazal after my heart goes full bloom,
Until then, with my pen scratching, keep patience

Let the aching hearts meet, let the lips open up
We will have all accounts settled, keep patiece

Look 'Nasir', nobody cares for others in this world
Forget those promises and vows, keep patience (12)

70. *rang barsaat ne bhare kuchh to*

rang barsaat ne bhare kuchh to
zakham dil ke huye hare kuchh to
fursat-e-bekhudi ganimat hai
gardishen ho gayeen pare kuchh to
kitane shorida-sar the parvaane
shaam hote hi jal mare kuchh to
aisaa mushkil nahin tera milnaa
dil magar justajoo kare kuchh to (4)
aao 'nasir' koyi ghazal chheden
jee bahal jaayega arre kuchh to

रंग बरसात ने भरे कुछ तो
ज़ख़्म दिल के हुए हरे कुछ तो
फ़ुर्सत-ए-बेख़ुदी ग़नीमत है
गर्दिशें हो गयीं परे कुछ तो
कितने शोरीदा-सर थे परवाने
शाम होते ही जल मरे कुछ तो
ऐसा मुश्किल नहीं तिरा मिलना
दिल मगर जुस्तजू करे कुछ तो (4)
आओ 'नासिर' कोई ग़ज़ल छेड़ें
जी बहल जाएगा अरे कुछ तो

70. The rain brought a cheer a little bit

The rain brought a cheer a little bit
Revived wounds of heart a little bit

Hard to free mind from blackouts
Though ordeals stayed away a little bit

They plunged into flames early evening*
Moths who were hot-headed a little bit

Not that hard it is to reach you, yet
Heart must make an effort a little bit (4)

'Nasir' let us have a ghazal going
That would delight our minds a little bit

*refers to the literary trope of an excited moth attracted to the flame (beloved)

71. rang dikhlati hai kya kya umr ki raftaar bhi

rang dikhlati hai kya kya umr ki raftaar bhi
baal chaandi ho gaye, sona hue rukhsaar bhi
dard ke jhonkon ne ab ki dil hi thanda kar diya
aag barsaata tha aage deeda-e-khoonbaar bhi
baithe-baithe jaane kyon betab ho jaata hai dil
puchhte kyaa ho miyan, achha bhi hoon bimaar bhi
shauq-e-azaadi liye jaata hai aalam se pare
rokati hai har qadam awaaz-e-paa-e-yaar bhi (4)
saadagi se tum na samjhe tark-e-duniya ka sabab
varna vo darvesh the parde men duniyadaar bhi
kis tarah guzrega 'nasir' fursat-e-hasti ka din
jam gayaa deewar ban kar saaya-e-deewar bhi

रंग दिखलाती है क्या-क्या उम्र की रफ़्तार भी
बाल चाँदी हो गये, सोना हुए रुख़सार भी
दर्द के झोंकों ने अबकी दिल ही ठण्डा कर दिया
आग बरसाता था आगे दीदा-ए-ख़ूँबार भी
बैठे-बैठे जाने क्यों बेताब हो जाता है दिल
पूछते क्या हो मियाँ, अच्छा भी हूँ, बीमार भी
शौक़-ए-आज़ादी लिए जाता है आलम से परे
रोकती है हर क़दम आवाज़-ए-पा-ए-यार भी (4)
सादगी से तुम न समझे तर्क़-ए-दुनिया का सबब
वरना वो दरवेश थे पर्दे में दुनियादार भी
किस तरह गुज़रेगा 'नासिर' फुर्सत-ए-हस्ती का दिन
जम गया दीवार बनकर साया-ए-दीवार भी

71. How many shades ageing shows in colour

How many shades ageing shows in colour
Silver in hair and cheeks in golden pallor

Every wave of pain now brings chill in heart
Earlier bleeding eye had fire in its shower

The heart goes restless even when at rest
'I am good, somewhat ill too', if you ask, sir

Love for freedom hastens me to another world
Sound of beloved's footsteps makes me slower (4)

Simplicity will not explain one's detachment
Saintly he was, but worldly too under cover

When will it end, 'Nasir, the grace period of life
Even the shadow of a wall is fixed now forever

72. raunaqen theen jahan men kya kya kuchh

raunaqen theen jahan men kya kya kuchh
log the raftagaan men kya kya kuchh
ab ki fasl-e-bahaar se pahle
rang the gulistan men kya kya kuchh
kya kahun ab tumhen khizaan vaalo
jal gaya aashiyan men kya kya kuchh
dil tere baad so gaya varna
shor tha is makan men kya kya kuchh (4)

रौनक़ें थीं जहाँ में क्या-क्या कुछ
लोग थे रफ़्तगाँ में क्या-क्या कुछ
अबकी फ़स्ल-ए-बहार से पहले
रंग थे गुलसिताँ में क्या-क्या कुछ
क्या कहूँ अब तुम्हें ख़िजाँ वालो
जल गया आशियाँ में क्या-क्या कुछ
दिल तिरे बाद सो गया वरना
शोर था इस मकाँ में क्या-क्या कुछ (4)

72. What joyous times the world had, imagine

What joyous times the world had, imagine
What wonderful souls once we had, imagine

Before the harvest of spring this season
What a resplendent garden we had, imagine

What can I tell you, the autumn lovers!
The losses in burnt nests we had, imagine

After you, the heart turned quiet, otherwise
What a furore this dwelling had, imagine (4)

73. *safar-e-manzil-e-shab yaad nahin*

safar-e-manzil-e-shab yaad nahin
log rukhsat hue kab yaad nahin
avvalin qurb ki sarshaari men
kitne armaan the jo ab yaad nahin
dil men har waqt chubhan rahti thi
thi mujhe kis ki talab yaad nahin
wo sitara thi ki shabnam thi ki phool
ek surat thi ajab yaad nahin (4)
kaisi viraan hai guzargah-e-khayal
jab se vo aariz o lab yaad nahin
bhulte jaate hain maazi ke dayaar
yaad aayen bhi to sab yaad nahin

सफ़र-ए-मंज़िल-ए-शब याद नहीं
लोग रुख़्सत हुए कब याद नहीं
अव्वलीं क़ुर्ब की सरशारी में
कितने अरमाँ थे जो अब याद नहीं
दिल में हर वक़्त चुभन रहती थी
थी मुझे किस की तलब याद नहीं
वो सितारा थी कि शबनम थी कि फूल
एक सूरत थी अजब याद नहीं (4)
कैसी वीराँ है गुज़र-गाह-ए-ख़याल
जब से वो आरिज़ ओ लब याद नहीं
भूलते जाते हैं माज़ी के दयार
याद आएँ भी तो सब याद नहीं

--continue--

73. The Night march to our post, I remember not

The Night march to our post, I remember not
When others left mid-way, I remember not

In that excitement, when we first got close
What longings I cherished, I remember not

In my heart I always had an aching urge
What exactly I hungered for, I remember not

Did it look like a star, a flower or a dew drop?
What a strange face it was, I remember not (4)

How deserted is the alley of my muse, since
Those cheeks and lips left, I remember not

I am slowly losing the memory of old places
Even if it comes back, all of it I remember not
                              --continue--

73. *safar-e-manzil-e-shab yaad nahin*

aisa uljha hun gham-e-duniya men
ek bhi khwab-e-tarab yaad nahin
rishta-e-jaan tha kabhi jis ka khayal
us ki surat bhi to ab yaad nahin (8)
ye haqeeqat hai ki ahbaab ko ham
yaad hi kab the jo ab yaad nahin
yaad hai sair-e-charaghan 'nasir'
dil ke bujhne ka sabab yaad nahin

ऐसा उलझा हूँ ग़म-ए-दुनिया में
एक भी ख़्वाब-ए-तरब याद नहीं
रिश्ता-ए-जाँ था कभी जिस का ख़याल
उस की सूरत भी तो अब याद नहीं (8)
ये हक़ीक़त है कि अहबाब को हम
याद ही कब थे जो अब याद नहीं
याद है सैर-ए-चराग़ाँ 'नासिर'
दिल के बुझने का सबब याद नहीं

73. The Night march to our post, I remember not

So much trapped I am in woes of the world
What rapturous dreams I had, I remember not

Whose memory I always held dear as life
Even a trace of her face now I remember not (8)

It is true friends were never really keen on me
Why should they miss me now, I remember not

Walks along rows of lights I remember, 'Nasir'
But why light blew out within, I remember not

74. sar men jab ishq ka sauda na raha

sar men jab ishq ka sauda na raha
kya kahen zeest men kya kya na raha
ab to duniya bhi vo duniya na rahi
ab tera dhyaan bhi utna na raha
qissa-e-shauq sunaun kis ko
raazdari ka zamana na raha
zindagi jis ki tamanna men kati
wo mere haal se begaana raha (4)
dere daale hain khizan ne chau-des
gul to gul baagh men kaanta na raha
din dahaade ye lahu ki holi
khalq ko khauf khuda ka na raha
ab to so jaao sitam ke maaro
aasman par koi taara na raha

सर में जब इश्क़ का सौदा न रहा
क्या कहें ज़ीस्त में क्या क्या न रहा
अब तो दुनिया भी वो दुनिया न रही
अब तिरा ध्यान भी उतना न रहा
क़िस्सा-ए-शौक़ सुनाऊँ किस को
राज़दारी का ज़माना न रहा
ज़िंदगी जिस की तमन्ना में कटी
वो मिरे हाल से बेगाना रहा (4)
डेरे डाले हैं ख़िज़ाँ ने चौ-देस
गुल तो गुल बाग़ में काँटा न रहा
दिन दहाड़े ये लहू की होली
ख़ल्क़ को ख़ौफ़ ख़ुदा का न रहा
अब तो सो जाओ सितम के मारो
आसमाँ पर कोई तारा न रहा

74. When the madness of love in me left

When the madness of love in me left
Can't tell what else in life with it left

I don't see the world now as it was once
Don't find you much in mind as I did once

Who shall I tell story of my love and desire
Little is left in world about care and share

All my life I longed for one in desperation
Who remained stranger to my emotion (4)

Autumn has set in all over the countryside
No flowers, not even thorns are in sight

In broad daylight, this parade of bloodbath
Do folks have no fear of God or his wrath

Victims of callousness better go to sleep
No star now in the sky for hope to keep

75. *saaz-e-hasti ki sadaa gaur se sun*

saaz-e-hasti ki sadaa ghaur se sun
kyun hai ye shor bapa ghaur se sun
din ke hangamon ko bekaar na jaan
shab ke pardon men hai kya ghaur se sun
chadhte suraj ki ada ko pahchaan
doobte din ki nida ghaur se sun
kyun thahr jaate hain dariya sar-e-sham
ruh ke taar hila ghaur se sun (4)
yaas ki chhanv men sone vaale
jaag aur shor-e-dara ghaur se sun
har-nafas dam-e-giraftaari hai
nau-giraftaar-e-bala ghaur se sun
dil tadap uthta hai kyun akhir-e-shab
do ghadi kaan laga ghaur se sun

साज़-ए-हस्ती की सदा ग़ौर से सुन
क्यों है ये शोर बपा, ग़ौर से सुन
दिन के हंगामों को बेकार न जान
शब के परदों में है क्या, ग़ौर से सुन
चढ़ते सूरज की अदा को पहचान
डूबते दिन की निदा, ग़ौर से सुन
क्यों ठहर जाते हैं दरिया सर-ए-शाम
रूह के तार हिला, ग़ौर से सुन (4)
यास की छाँव में सोने वाले
जाग और शोर-ए-दरा ग़ौर से सुन
हर नफ़स दाम-ए-गिरफ़्तारी है
नौ-गिरफ़्तार-ए-बला, ग़ौर से सुन
दिल तड़प उठता है क्यूँ आख़िर-ए-शब
दो घड़ी कान लगा, ग़ौर से सुन

--continue--

75. The ringing call of life, listen with care

The ringing call of life, listen with care
Why this uproar around, listen with care

Don't you take the daytime mayhem lightly
What lies behind the night, listen with care

See the promise that the rising sun makes
The plea of the dying day, listen with care

Why do rivers calm down by the sunset?
strum the strings of soul, listen with care (4)

You who sleep under the shade of sorrows
Rise, hour-gong is ringing, listen with care

Each moment is a hunter's net to trap you
Those new to misfortunes, listen with care

Why does it shudder in last hours of night
Put your ears to your heart, listen with care
                                --continue--

75. saaz-e-hasti ki sadaa gaur se sun

isi manzil men hain sab hijr-o-visal
rahrav-e-aabla paa ghaur se sun (8)
isi goshe men hain sab dair-o-haram
dil sanam hai ki khuda ghaur se sun
kaaba sunsan hai kyun ai vaaiz
haath kanon se utha ghaur se sun
maut aur zeest ke asraar-e-rumuz
aa meri bazm men aa ghaur se sun
kya guzarti hai kisi ke dil par
tu bhi ai jaan-e-wafa ghaur se sun (12)
kabhi fursat ho to ai subah-e-jamaal
shab-gazidon ki dua ghaur se sun

इसी मंज़िल में हैं सब हिज्र-ओ-विसाल
रहरव-ए-आबला-पा, ग़ौर से सुन (8)
इसी गोशे में हैं सब दैर-ओ-हरम
दिल सनम है कि ख़ुदा, ग़ौर से सुन
काबा सुनसान है क्यों ऐ वाइज़
हाथ कानों से उठा, ग़ौर से सुन
मौत और ज़ीस्त के असरार-ओ-रमुज
आ मेरी बज़्म में आ, ग़ौर से सुन
क्या गुज़रती है किसी के दिल पर
तू भी ऐ जान-ए-वफ़ा, ग़ौर से सुन (12)
कभी फ़ुरसत हो तो ऐ सुब्ह-ए-जमाल
शबगज़ीदों की दुआ, ग़ौर से सुन

75. The ringing call of life, listen with care

All partings and meetings find an end here
Walkers with bruised soles, listen with care (8)

Lodged in this nook is a temple, a mosque
Is your heart an idol or God, listen with care

Why is there no one in the mosque, cleric?
Take your hands off your ears, listen with care

Of meaning and mystery of life and death
Come to my gathering and listen with care

what does an afflicted heart go through
You too, the love of my life, listen with care (12)

Whenever free, Oh, morning-faced beauty
Prayers of the night-bittens, listen with care

76. *shahr-dar-shahr ghar jalaaye gaye*

shahr-dar-shahr ghar jalaaye gaye
yun bhi jashn-e-tarab manaaye gaye
ik taraf jhoom kar bahaar aayee
ik taraf aashiyaan jalaaye gaye
kyaa kahoon kis tarah sar-e-bazaar
ismaton ke diye bujhaaye gaye
aah vo khilvaton ke saramaaye
majama-e-aam men lutaaye gaye (4)
waqt ke saath ham bhi ai 'nasir'
khaar-o-khas ki tarah bahaaye gaye

शहर-दर-शहर घर जलाये गये
यूँ भी जश्न-ए-तरब मनाये गये
इक तरफ़ झूम कर बहार आयी
इक तरफ़ आशियाँ जलाये गये
क्या कहूँ किस तरह सर-ए-बाज़ार
इस्मतों के दिये बुझाये गये
आह वो ख़िल्वतों के सरमाये
मजमा-ए-आम में लुटाए गये (4)
वक़्त के साथ हम भी ऐ 'नासिर'
ख़ार-ओ-ख़स की तरह बहाए गये

76. Cities after cities, homes were set on fire

Cities after cities, homes were set on fire
That's how festivities were made there

Here the spring swings in with blossoms
Over there the nests were razed in a flare

What can I say how in the broad daylight
Honour and dignity were made to despair

The much treasured secrets of privacy
Alas! were publically blown up in the air (4)

The torrent of time in its mighty onslaught
Dumped us too like weedy trash, 'Nasir'

77. shahr sunsaan hai kidhar jaayen

shahr sunsaan hai kidhar jaayen
khaak ho kar kahin bikhar jaayen
raat kitni guzar gayi lekin
itni himmat nahin ki ghar jaayen
yun tere dhyaan se larazta hun
jaise patte hava se dar jaayen
un ujaalon ki dhun men phirta hun
chhab dikhaate hi jo guzar jaayen (4)
rain andheri hai aur kinaara door
chand nikle to paar utar jaayen

शहर सुनसान है किधर जाएँ
ख़ाक होकर कहीं बिखर जाएँ
रात कितनी गुज़र गई लेकिन
इतनी हिम्मत नहीं कि घर जाएँ
यूँ तेरे ध्यान से लरज़ता हूँ
जैसे पत्ते हवा से डर जाएँ
उन उजालों की धुन में फिरता हूँ
छब दिखाते ही जो गुज़र जाएँ (4)
रैन अँधेरी है और किनारा दूर
चाँद निकले तो पार उतर जाएँ

77. The town is desolate, where can I go

The town is desolate, where can I go
Like dust, shouldn't I scatter and blow

Night has passed well into late hours
I don't have the nerve for home to go

A thought of you gives my heart a quiver
Like leaves flutter when the winds blow

I am earnestly looking for those lights
That fade away as soon as they glow (4)

The night is dark and far is the coast
We can make it if the moon shows up now

78. *shuaan-e-husn tere husn ko chhupaati thi*

shuaan-e-husn tere husn ko chhupaati thi
vo roshani thi ki soorat nazar na aati thi
kise milen, kahan jaayen ki raat kaali hai
vo shakl hi na rahi jo diye jalaati thi
vo hi to din the haqeeqat men umr ka haasil
khusha vo din ki hamen roz maut aati thi
zara see baat se hi tera yaad aa jaana
zara see baat bahut der tak rulaati thi (4)
udaas baithe ho kyoon haath tod kar 'nasir'
vo nai kahan hai jo taaron kee neend udaati thi

शुआ-ए-हुस्न तिरे हुस्न को छुपाती थी
वो रोशनी थी कि सूरत नज़र न आती थी
किसे मिलें, कहाँ जाएँ कि रात काली है
वो शक्ल ही न रही जो दिये जलाती थी
वो ही तो दिन थे हक़ीक़त में उम्र का हासिल
ख़ुशा वो दिन कि हमें रोज़ मौत आती थी
ज़रा-सी बात से ही तेरा याद आ जाना
ज़रा-सी बात बहुत देर तक रुलाती थी (4)
उदास बैठे हो क्यूँ हाथ तोड़ कर 'नासिर'
वो नै कहाँ है जो तारों की नींद उड़ाती थी

78. Glowing rays of beauty veiled your visage

Glowing rays of beauty veiled your visage
Radiance was too much to see your image

Where to go, who to meet, in this dark night
We have lost the one who lighted our passage

Those days were indeed the gain of all my life
When happily I dared death at every stage

How the little things made me remember you
How for long in tears they held me hostage (4)

Why sit in gloom with your hands idle 'Nasir'
Where is the flute that halted the stars' voyage

79. *so gayi shahr ki har ek gali*

so gayi shahr ki har ek gali
ab to aaja ki raat bheeg chali
koyi jhonkaa chala to dil dhadka
dil dhadkate hi teri yaad aayi
kaun hai tu, kahaan se aaya hai
kahin dekha hai tujhko pehle bhi
tu bata, kyaa tujhe savaab mila
khair main ne to raat kaat hi li (4)
mujh se kya puchhta hai mera haal
saamne hai tere kitaab khuli
mere dil se na jaa khuda ke liye
aisi basti na phir basegi kabhi

सो गई शहर की हर एक गली
अब तो आ-जा कि रात भीग चली
कोई झोंका चला तो दिल धड़का
दिल धड़कते ही तेरी याद आयी
कौन है तू, कहाँ से आया है
कहीं देखा है तुझको पहले भी
तू बता, क्या तुझे सवाब मिला
ख़ैर मैंने तो रात काट ही ली (4)
मुझसे क्या पूछता है मेरा हाल
सामने है तिरे किताब खुली
मेरे दिल से न जा खुदा के लिए
ऐसी बस्ती न फिर बसेगी कभी
--continue--

79. The city is asleep so is its every street

The city is asleep so is its every street
Night is getting dewy, come and meet

A gust of wind and my heart skips a beat
With heartbeat, memories of you repeat

Who are you, where do you come from?
I seem to have seen you before this meet

Tell me, did you have some good time
As for my night I just managed to beat (4)

What do you want to know about me
It is an open book in front of you to read

For God's sake, don't you leave my heart
It will never come to life again, I entreat
                                    --continue--

79. so gayi shahr ki har ek gali

main isi gham men ghulta jaata hoon
kya mujhe chhod jaayega tu bhi
aisi jaldi bhi kya chale jaana
mujhe ik baat puchhni hai abhi(8)
aa bhi jaa mere dil ke sadranashin
kab se khaali padi hai ye kursi
main to halkaan ho gaya 'nasir'
muddat-e-hijr kitani phail gayi

मैं इसी ग़म में घुलता जाता हूँ
क्या मुझे छोड़ जायेगा तू भी
ऐसी जल्दी भी क्या चले जाना
मुझे इक बात पूछनी है अभी (8)
आ भी जा मेरे दिल के सद्रनशीं
कब से ख़ाली पड़ी है ये कुर्सी
मैं तो हल्कान हो गया 'नासिर'
मुद्दत-ए-हिज्र कितनी फैल गयी

79. The city is asleep so is its every street

This worry alone is eating into my heart
That like others you too would retreat

Where is the hurry, why leave so soon?
I have yet to ask you something sweet (8)

Come, take over, the ruler of my heart
For long have I left vacant this loveseat

I am utterly crushed and beaten 'Nasir'
This spell of parting will never recede

80. sunaata hai koyi bhooli kahani

sunaata hai koyi bhooli kahaani
mahakte mithe dariyaon ka paani
yahan jangal the abadi se pehle
suna hai main ne logon ki zabaani
yahan ik shahr tha shahr-e-nigaaraan
na chhodi waqt ne us ki nishaani
main vo dil hun dabistan-e-alam ka
jise royegi sadiyon shadmaani (4)
tasavvur ne use dekha hai aksar
khirad kahti hai jis ko lamakaani
khayalon hi men aksar baithe baithe
basa leta hun ik duniya suhaani

सुनाता है कोई भूली कहानी
महकते मीठे दरियाओं का पानी
यहाँ जंगल थे आबादी से पहले
सुना है मैंने लोगों की ज़बानी
यहाँ इक शहर था शहर-ए-निग़ाराँ
न छोड़ी वक़्त ने उसकी कहानी
मैं वो दिल हूँ दबिस्तान-ए-अलम का
जिसे रोयेगी सदियों शादमानी (4)
तसव्वुर ने उसे देखा है अक्सर
ख़िरद कहती है जिसको लामकानी
ख़यालों ही में अक्सर बैठे-बैठे
बसा लेता हूँ इक दुनिया सुहानी
--continue--

80. Someone tells a tale long lost

Someone tells a tale long lost
Of rivers and waters sweet most

We had woods where we now dwell
I have heard it say when people tell

Here was a town of beauty and grace
But time has spared none of its trace

I am the soul of the school of distress
That goodtimes will for years miss (4)

Imagination has witnessed its visual
What intellect calls simply mystical

Sitting and reflecting often in leisure
I create a world of my own pleasure
      --continue--

80. sunaata hai koyi bhooli kahani

hujum-e-nasha-e-fikr-e-sukhan men
badal jaate hain lafzon ke maani
bata ai zulmat-e-sahra-e-imkaan
kahan hoga mere khwaabon ka saani (8)
andheri shaam ke pardon men chhup kar
kise roti hai chashmon ki ravaani
kiran pariyan utarti hain kahan se
kahan jaate hain raste kahkashaani
pahadon se chali phir koyi aandhi
ude jaate hain auraq-e-khizaani
nai duniya ke hangamon men 'nasir'
dabi jaati hain awaazen puraani (12)

हुजूम-ए-नश्शा-ए-फ़िक्र-ए-सुख़न में
बदल जाते हैं लफ़्ज़ों के मआनी
बता ऐ ज़ुल्मत-ए-सहरा-ए-इमकाँ
कहाँ होगा मेरे ख़्वाबों का सानी (8)
अंधेरी शाम के पर्दा में छुप कर
किसे रोती है चश्मों की रवानी
किरनपरियाँ उतरती हैं कहाँ से
कहाँ जाते हैं रस्ते कहकशानी
पहाड़ों से चली फिर कोई आँधी
उड़े जाते हैं औराक़-ए-ख़िजानी
नयी दुनिया के हंगामों में 'नासिर'
दबी जाती हैं आवाज़ें पुरानी (12)

80. Someone tells a tale long lost

In the heady rush of poetic musings
Words undergo a change in meanings

Tell me, O hoary desert of possibilities
Where is the match for my fantasies? (8)

Hidden under the pall of a dark evening
Who the waterfall mourns in its wailing

Wherefrom the light fairies descend
Where do the trails of milkyways end?

In the sweep of a fresh mountain gust
The autumn leaves are smitten to dust

In the clamour of the new world, 'Nasir'
Old voices are coming under pressure (12)

81. tanhai ka dukh gahra tha

tanhai ka dukh gahra tha
main dariya dariya rota tha
ek hi lahar na sambhali varna
main tufaanon se khela tha
tanhai ka tanha saaya
der se mere saath laga tha
chhod gaye jab saare sathi
tanhai ne saath diya tha (4)
sookh gayi jab sukh ki daali
tanhai ka phool khila tha

तन्हाई का दुख गहरा था
मैं दरिया दरिया रोता था
एक ही लहर न संभली वर्ना
मैं तूफ़ानों से खेला था
तन्हाई का तन्हा साया
देर से मेरे साथ लगा था
छोड़ गए जब सारे साथी
तन्हाई ने साथ दिया था (4)
सूख गई जब सुख की डाली
तन्हाई का फूल खिला था
--continue--

81. The pain of loneliness was deep set

The pain of loneliness was deep set
Rivers of tears, my eyes would get

I could not handle one major tide
Otherwise many a storm I have met

This singular phantom of loneliness
Had for long trapped me in its net

When everbody had drifted away
It was loneliness that never left (4)

When every shoot of joy dried up
Loneliness would grow into a floret
                    --continue--

81. tanhai ka dukh gahra tha

tanhai men yad-e-k̲huda thi
tanhai men khauf-e-k̲huda tha
tanhai mehrab-e-ibaadat
tanhai mimbar ka diya tha
tanhai mera paa-e-shikasta
tanhai mera dast-e-dua tha (8)
vo jannat mere dil men chhupi thi
main jise bahar dhund raha tha
tanhai mere dil ki jannat
main tanha hun main tanha tha

तन्हाई में याद-ए-ख़ुदा थी
तन्हाई में ख़ौफ़-ए-ख़ुदा था
तन्हाई मेहराब-ब-इबादत
तन्हाई मिम्बर का दिया था
तन्हाई मिरा पा-ए-शिकस्ता
तन्हाई मिरा दस्त-ए-दुआ था (8)
वो जन्नत मिरे दिल में छुपी थी
मैं जिसे बाहर ढूँड रहा था
तन्हाई मिरे दिल की जन्नत
मैं तन्हा हूँ मैं तन्हा था

81. The pain of loneliness was deep set

In loneliness, I remembered God
His wrath too, I could not forget

Loneliness, the arch of my faith
It was also the light on my pulpit

Loneliness gave me broken feet
But hands too that in prayer met (8)

Inside my heart sat that bliss which
I had sought outside at the outset

Loneliness is a heaven in my heart
I was all by myself and I am so yet

82. tere aane ka dhoka sa raha hai

tere aane ka dhoka sa raha hai
diya sa raat bhar jalta raha hai
ajab hai raat se aankhon ka aalam
ye dariya raat bhar chadhta raha hai
suna hai raat bhar barsa hai badal
magar vo shahr jo pyaasa raha hai
vo koyi dost tha achhe dinon ka
jo pichhli raat se yaad aa raha hai (4)
kise dhundoge in galiyon men 'nasir'
chalo ab ghar chalen din ja raha hai

तिरे आने का धोखा-सा रहा है
दिया-सा रात भर जलता रहा है
अजब है रात से आँखों का आलम
ये दरिया रात भर चढ़ता रहा है
सुना है रात भर बरसा है बादल
मगर वो शहर जो प्यासा रहा है
वो कोई दोस्त था अच्छे दिनों का
जो पिछली रात से याद आ रहा है (4)
किसे ढूँढोगे इन गलियों में 'नासिर'
चलो अब घर चलें, दिन जा रहा है

82. I had a faint idea of your coming

I had a faint idea of your coming
All night I kept a lamp burning

Strange is the feeling in these eyes
From last night a river seems rising

Seems we had heavy rains last night
What about that city left thirsting

He must be a friend of good old days
Who from last night I've been missing (4)

Who'd you find in these streets, 'Nasir'
Let's get back home, the day is dying

83. tere khayaal se lo de uthi hai tanhai

tere khayaal se lo de uthi hai tanhai
shab-e-firaq hai ya teri jalwa aarai
tu kis khayaal men hai manzilon ke shaidai
unhen bhi dekh jinhen raaste men neend aai
pukar ai jars-e-kaarvan-e-subah-e-tarb
bhatak rahe hain andheron men tere saudai
thahar gaye hain sar-e-raah khaak udaane ko
musafiron ko na chhed ai hava-e-sahrai (4)
rah-e-hayat men kuchh marhale to dekh liye
ye aur baat teri aarzoo na raas aai
ye saaneha bhi mohabbat men barha guzra
ki us ne haal bhi puchha to aankh bhar aai

तिरे ख़याल से लो दे उठी है तन्हाई
शब-ए-फ़िराक़ है या तेरी जल्वा-आराई
तू किस ख़याल में है मंज़िलों के शैदाई
उन्हें भी देख जिन्हें रास्ते में नींद आई
पुकार ऐ जरस-ए-कारवान-ए-सुब्ह-ए-तरब
भटक रहे हैं अंधेरों में तेरे सौदाई
ठहर गए हैं सर-ए-राह ख़ाक उड़ाने को
मुसाफ़िरों को न छेड़ ऐ हवा-ए-सहराई (4)
रह-ए-हयात में कुछ मरहले तो देख लिए
ये और बात तिरी आरज़ू न रास आई
ये सानेहा भी मोहब्बत में बार-हा गुज़रा
कि उस ने हाल भी पूछा तो आँख भर आई

--continue--

83. A flashback of you has lit up my solitary existence

A flashback of you has lit up my solitary existence
Is it a lonely night or a celebration of your presence

What is it that drives you mad about journey's end
Think of those who went into last sleep on the bend

Ring the caravan bell to herald dawn of a new day
In the darkness, your followers have gone astray

They stopped on the way, just to hang out in dust
O desert winds! don't grudge the travellers in rest (4)

On the highway of life, I have managed a few crises
Though your love is something I could never harness

A disaster like this has happened in love too often
When eyes well up at a chance greeting of someone

--continue--

83. tere khayaal se lo de uthi hai tanhai

dil-e-fasurda men phir dhadkanon ka shor utha
ye baithe baithe mujhe kin dinon ki yaad aai
main sote sote kayi baar chaunk chaunk pada
tamaam raat tere pahluon se aanch aai (8)
jahan bhi tha koyi fitna tadap ke jaag utha
tamaam hosh thi masti men teri angdaai
khuli jo aankh to kuchh aur hi samaan dekha
vo log the na vo jalse na shahr-e-raanaai
vo taab-e-dard vo sauda-e-intizaar kahan
unhi ke saath gayi taqat-e-shakebaai
phir us ki yaad men dil beqaraar hai 'nasir'
bichhad ke jis se huyi shahr shahr rusvaai (12)

दिल-ए-फ़सुर्दा में फिर धड़कनों का शोर उठा
ये बैठे बैठे मुझे किन दिनों की याद आई
मैं सोते सोते कई बार चौंक चौंक पड़ा
तमाम रात तिरे पहलुओं से आँच आई (8)
जहाँ भी था कोई फ़ित्ना तड़प के जाग उठा
तमाम होश थी मस्ती में तेरी अंगड़ाई
खुली जो आँख तो कुछ और ही समाँ देखा
वो लोग थे न वो जलसे न शहर-ए-रानाई
वो ताब-ए-दर्द वो सौदा-ए-इंतिज़ार कहाँ
उन्ही के साथ गई ताक़त-ए-शकेबाई
फिर उस की याद में दिल बे-क़रार है 'नासिर'
बिछड़ के जिस से हुई शहर शहर रुस्वाई (12)

83. A flashback of you has lit up my solitary existence

My sick heart suddenly had an uproar of heartbeat
Is the turbulence of some old days going to repeat?

Many times did I jump out of sleep with a fright
A warmth from your side I felt rising all night (8)

An uprising wherever it was sprang to life for fun
On seeing a naughty move in your seductive turn

When my eyes opened it was a different spectacle
I saw nothing of the old city, its folks or its sparkle

Where is tenacity for pain or whim of persistence
It vanished with old mates, this power of patience

Once again the heart is getting restless missing her
Who left me humiliated all over the place 'Nasir'   (12)

84. tere milne ko bekal ho gaye hain

tere milne ko bekal ho gaye hain
magar ye log paagal ho gaye hain
bahaaren le ke aaye the jahan tum
vo ghar sunsaan jangal ho gaye hain
yahan tak badh gaye alaam-e-hasti
ki dil ke hausle shal ho gaye hain
kahan tak taab laaye naatavan dil
ki sadme ab musalsal ho gaye hain (4)
nigah-e-yaas ko neend aa rahi hai
mizha par ashk bojhal ho gaye hain
unhen sadiyon na bhulega zamana
yahan jo hadse kal ho gaye hain
jinhen ham dekh kar jeete the 'nasir'
vo log aankhon se ojhal ho gaye hain

तिरे मिलने को बेकल हो गये हैं
मगर ये लोग पागल हो गये हैं
बहारें ले के आए थे जहाँ तुम
वो घर सुनसान जंगल हो गए हैं
यहाँ तक बढ़ गए आलाम-ए-हस्ती
कि दिल के हौंसले शल हो गए हैं
कहाँ तक ताब लाए नातवाँ दिल
कि सदमे अब मुसलसल हो गए हैं (4)
निगाह-ए-यास को नींद आ रही है
मिज़ह पर अश्क बोझल हो गए हैं
उन्हें सदियों न भूलेगा ज़माना
यहाँ जो हादिसे कल हो गए हैं
जिन्हें हम देखकर जीते थे 'नासिर'
वो लोग आँखों से ओझल हो गए हैं

84. To meet you they seem to be excited

To meet you they seem to be excited
But they look somewhat insane about it

Those homes where you brought spring
Have now grown wild and desolate

Life's miseries have multiplied so much
Even the will to fight them has wilted

How long can a weak heart shore up
Not a day passes without a shock to it (4)

Eyes in depression are getting drowsy
Tears are sitting heavy on the eyelid

The havoc we saw here the other day
Would take the people eons to forget it

Those who we were our lifeline, 'Nasir'
Have suddenly left us in the middle of it.

85. *teri nigah ke jaadu bikharte jaate hain*

teri nigah ke jaadu bikharte jaate hain
jo zakhm dil ko mile the vo bharte jaate hain
tere baghair vo din bhi guzar gaye aakhir
tere baghair ye din bhi guzarte jaate hain
liye chalo mujhe dariya-e-shauq ki maujo
ki hamsafar to mere paar utarte jaate hain
tamam-umr jahan hanste khelte guzri
ab us gali men bhi ham darte darte jaate hain (4)
main khwahishon ke gharaunde banaye jaata hun
vo mehnaten meri barbad karte jaate hain

तिरी निगाह के जादू बिखरते जाते हैं
जो ज़ख़्म दिल को मिले थे वो भरते जाते हैं
तिरे बग़ैर वो दिन भी गुज़र गये आख़िर
तिरे बग़ैर ये दिन भी गुज़रते जाते हैं
लिए चलो मुझे दरिया-ए-शौक़ की मौजों
कि हमसफ़र तो मिरे पार उतरते जाते हैं
तमाम उम्र जहाँ हँसते-खेलते गुज़री
अब उस गली में भी हम डरते-डरते जाते हैं (4)
मैं ख़्वाहिशों के घरौंदे बनाये जाता हूँ
वो मेहनतें मेरी बर्बाद करते जाते हैं

85. The magic of your eyes has started fading

The magic of your eyes has started fading
The lesions in my heart have started healing

Days without you did pass off in the past
Days without you now as well are rolling

Waves of the sea of my passion! carry me on
While my friends crossed over to the landing

The street where I spent all my years in gaiety
Is the one that looks to me now so forbidding (4)

I keep building little shelters for my longings
She keeps shattering them by demolishing

86. teri zulfon ke bikharne ka sabab hai koyi

teri zulfon ke bikharne ka sabab hai koyi
aankh kahti hai tere dil men talab hai koyi
aanch aati hai tere jism ki uryani se
pairahan hai ki sulagti hui shab hai koyi
hosh udaane lagin phir chand ki thandi kiranen
teri basti men hun ya khwab-e-tarab hai koyi
geet bunti hai tere shahr ki bharpur hava
ajnabi main hi nahin tu bhi ajab hai koyi (4)
liye jaati hain kisi dhyaan ki lahren 'nasir'
door tak silsila-e-taak-e-tarab hai koyi

तेरी जुल्फ़ों के बिखरने का सबब है कोई
आँख कहती है तिरे दिल में तलब है कोई
आँच आती है तिरे जिस्म की उर्यानी से
पैरहन है कि सुलगती हुई शब है कोई
होश उड़ाने लगीं फिर चाँद की ठंडी किरनें
तेरी बस्ती में हूँ या ख़्वाब-ए-तरब है कोई
गीत बुनती है तिरे शहर की भरपूर हवा
अजनबी मैं ही नहीं तू भी अजब है कोई (4)
लिए जाती हैं किसी ध्यान की लहरें 'नासिर'
दूर तक सिलसिला-ए-ताक-ए-तरब है कोई

86. Not for nothing you have ruffled hair

Not for nothing you have ruffled hair
Your eyes speak of some hidden desire

Heat emanates from your naked body
Is it your nightgown or the night on fire

The cool rays of moon are making me dizzy
Am I at your abode or at a fantasy funfair

The air of your town weaves a music
Not me, you too look a bit stranger here (4)

Fancy feelings keep pushing me on 'Nasir'
Spread afar are the stretches of pleasure

87. *tu asir-e-bazm hai ham-sukhan*

tu asir-e-bazm hai ham-sukhan tujhe zauq-e-nala-e-nai nahin
tera dil gudaaz ho kis tarah ye tire mizaaj ki lai nahin
tera har kamaal hai zaahiri tera har khayaal hai sarsari
koyi dil ki baat karun to kya tere dil men aag to hai nahin
jise sun ke ruh mahak uthe jise pee ke dard chahak uthe
tere saaz men vo sadaa nahin tere maikade men vo mai nahin
kahan ab vo mausam-e-rang-o-bu ki ragon men bol uthe lahu
yun hi nagavaar chubhan si hai ki jo shamil-e-rag-o-pai nahin (4)
tera dil ho dard se aashna to ye naala ghaur se sun zara
bada jan-gusil hai ye vaqia ye fasaana-e-jam-o-kai nahin
main hun ek shair-e-benava mujhe kaun chahe mere siva
main amir-e-sham-o-ajam nahin main kabir-e-kufa-o-rai nahin
yahi sher hain meri saltanat isi fan men hai mujhe aafiyat
mere kasa-e-shab-o-roz men tere kaam ki koyi shai nahin

तू असीर-ए-बज़्म है हम-सुख़न तुझे ज़ौक़-ए-नाला-ए-नय नहीं
तिरा दिल गुदाज़ हो किस तरह ये तिरे मिज़ाज की लय नहीं
तिरा हर कमाल है ज़ाहिरी तिरा हर ख़याल है सरसरी
कोई दिल की बात करूँ तो क्या तिरे दिल में आग तो है नहीं
जिसे सुन के रूह महक उठे जिसे पी के दर्द चहक उठे
तिरे साज़ में वो सदा नहीं तिरे मय-कदे में वो मय नहीं
कहाँ अब वो मौसम-ए-रंग-ओ-बू कि रगों में बोल उठे लहू
यूँही नागवार चुभन सी है कि जो शामिल-ए-रग-ओ-पै नहीं (4)
तिरा दिल हो दर्द से आश्ना तो ये नाला ग़ौर से सुन ज़रा
बड़ा जाँ-गुसिल है ये वाक़िआ ये फ़साना-ए-जम-ओ-कै नहीं
मैं हूँ एक शाइर-ए-बे-नवा मुझे कौन चाहे मिरे सिवा
मैं अमीर-ए-शाम-ओ-अजम नहीं मैं कबीर-ए-कूफ़ा-ओ-रै नहीं
यही शेर हैं मिरी सल्तनत इसी फ़न में है मुझे आफ़ियत
मिरे कासा-ए-शब-ओ-रोज़ में तिरे काम की कोई शय नहीं

87. O friend, you are a captive of your camp

O friend, you are a captive of your camp,
unaware of the song of flute
How can your heart be receptive
when your temperament does not suit

You excel in what is obvious,
the train of your thought is on lines casual
How can I connect with you
when in your heart there is no fire in actual

The song that elates the soul,
the drink that gives voice to a heartburn
There is no such music in your harmonica,
no such wine in your tavern

Where is that season of colour or odour
that makes the blood scream
What you have is a trifling pain t
hat does not arouse the blood stream (4)

If your heart understands pain,
then listen closely to this tortured strain
It is an act of self-decimation
not a tale about some old Persian sovereign

I am a poet of limited means and talent,
who will listen to me except me
I am not a ruler of Arab territories
or a noble from the land of Kufa or Ray[*]

My verses are my estate, my joy too,
with this art alone I make do
What I have in my bowl from day and night
is hardly of any use to you

[*] old Sultanates in Iran

88. tujh bin ghar kitna soona tha

tujh bin ghar kitna soona tha
deewaron se dar lagta tha
bhooli nahin vo sham-e-judaai
main us roz bahut roya tha
tujh ko jaane ki jaldi thi
aur main tujh ko rok raha tha
meri ankhen bhi roti theen
shaam ka taara bhi rota tha
galiyan shaam se bujhi bujhi theen
chand bhi jaldi doob gaya tha
sannate men jaise koi
door se awaazen deta tha
yadon ki sidhi se 'nasir'
raat ik saaya sa utra tha

तुझ बिन घर कितना सूना था
दीवारों से डर लगता था
भूली नहीं वो शाम-ए-जुदाई
मैं उस रोज़ बहुत रोया था
तुझ को जाने की जल्दी थी
और मैं तुझ को रोक रहा था
मेरी आँखें भी रोती थीं
शाम का तारा भी रोता था (4)
गलियाँ शाम से बुझी बुझी थीं
चाँद भी जल्दी डूब गया था
सन्नाटे में जैसे कोई
दूर से आवाज़ें देता था
यादों की सीढ़ी से 'नासिर'
रात इक साया सा उतरा था

88. How bleak was home without you

How bleak was home without you
The walls gave me real fright

I can't forget the eve we parted
On that day how much I cried

You were in a hurry to leave,
To stop you from going I tried

My eyes shed a lot of tears
And the evening star too cried (4)

Streets were soaked in dim light
Early that evening moon too died

In the still darkness someone, as if
From far away, called me aside

From the mind's staircase 'Nasir'
I saw at night a shadow glide

89. *tum aa gaye ho to kyun intizaar-e-shaam karen*

tum aa gaye ho to kyun intizaar-e-shaam karen
kaho to kyun na abhi se kuchh ehtimaam karen
khulus-o-mehr-o-wafa log kar chuke hain bahut
mere khayal men ab aur koyi kaam karen
ye khas-o-aam ki bekar guftugu kab tak
qubool ki jiye jo faisla awaam karen
har aadmi nahin shaista-e-rumooz-e-sukhan
vo kamsukhan ho mukhatab to hamkalaam karen (4)
juda hue hain bahut log ek tum bhi sahi
ab itni baat pe kya zindagi haraam karen
khuda agar kabhi kuchh ikhtiyaar de ham ko
tu pahle khak-nashinon ka intizaam karen
rah-e-talab men jo gumnaam mar gaye 'nasir'
mataa-e-dard unhi sathiyon ke naam karen

तुम आ गए हो तो क्यूँ इंतिज़ार-ए-शाम करें
कहो तो क्यूँ न अभी से कुछ एहतिमाम करें
ख़ुलूस-ओ-मेहर-ओ-वफ़ा लोग कर चुके हैं बहुत
मिरे ख़याल में अब और कोई काम करें
ये ख़ास-ओ-आम की बेकार गुफ़्तुगू कब तक
कुबूल कीजिए जो फ़ैसला अवाम करें
हर आदमी नहीं शाइस्ता-ए-रुमूज़-ए-सुख़न
वो कम-सुख़न हो मुख़ातब तो हम-कलाम करें (4)
जुदा हुए हैं बहुत लोग एक तुम भी सही
अब इतनी बात पे क्या ज़िंदगी हराम करें
ख़ुदा अगर कभी कुछ इख़्तियार दे हम को
तू पहले ख़ाक-नशीनों का इंतिज़ाम करें
रह-ए-तलब में जो गुमनाम मर गए 'नासिर'
मता-ए-दर्द उन्ही साथियों के नाम करें

89. Since you are here, why wait for the evening

Since you are here, why wait for the evening
If you please, can we arrange for something

Enough of love, grace, sincerity, we have had
It is time now, besides that, we do something

Why have this futile debate on high and low
Let us accept what comes as people's ruling

Not all are familiar with subtleties of poetry
With a less articulate, we choose speaking (4)

So many have deserted, let you be one of them
For this alone I will not let my life to grieving

If God ever grants me some control over things
To the lowly ones, I will first provide something

All who died on way to their mission unbeknown
Let's dedicate them 'Nasir' this saga of suffering

90. vo dil-nawaaz hai lekin nazar-shanaas nahin

vo dil-nawaaz hai lekin nazar-shanaas nahin
mera ilaaj mere charagar ke paas nahin
tadap rahe hain zaban par kayi sawaal magar
mere liye koyi shayan-e-iltimaas nahin
tere jilau men bhi dil kaamp kaamp uthta hai
mere mizaj ko aasoodgi bhi raas nahin
kabhi kabhi jo tere qurb men guzare the
ab un dinon ka tasavvur bhi mere paas nahin (4)
guzar rahe hain ajab marhalon se deeda-o-dil
sahar ki aas to hai zindagi ki aas nahin
mujhe ye dar hai teri aarzoo na mit jaaye
bahut dinon se tabiyat meri udaas nahin

वो दिल नवाज़ है लेकिन नज़र-शनास नहीं
मिरा इलाज मिरे चारागर के पास नहीं
तड़प रहे हैं ज़बाँ पर कई सवाल मगर
मेरे लिए कोई शायान-ए-इल्तिमास नहीं
तिरे जिलौ में भी दिल काँप-काँप उठता है
मिरे मिज़ाज को आसूदगी भी रास नहीं
कभी-कभी जो तेरे कुर्ब में गुज़ारे थे
अब उन दिनों का तसव्वुर भी मेरे पास नहीं (4)
गुज़र रहे हैं अजब मरहलों से दीदा-ओ-दिल
सहर की आस तो है, ज़िंदगी की आस नहीं
मुझे ये डर है तेरी आरज़ू न मिट जाये
बहुत दिनों से तबीयत मेरी उदास नहीं

90. He can console but not read eyes and tell

He can console but not read eyes and tell
My doctor knows not what will get me well

There are questions writhing on my tongue
Who should I ask, is there a capable one?

Even on a royal steed my heart goes down
I am not used to the luxuries of the crown

The few moments close to you that I spent
Are gone forever leaving no trace or scent (4)

Going by these terrible times, the heart may
Survive for a day but surely not all the way

My longing for you is nearing an end, I fear
For days I have not felt sad or low on cheer

91. *vo is ada se jo aaye to kyun bhala na lage*

vo is ada se jo aaye to kyun bhala na lage
hazaar baar milo phir bhi aashna na lage
kabhi vo khaas inaayat ki sau gumaan guzren
kabhi vo tarz-e-taghaful ki mujrimana lage
vo sidhi sadi adayen ki bijliyan barsen
vo dilbaraana muravvat ki aashiqana lage
dikhaun dagh-e-mohabbat jo nagavaar na ho
sunaun qissa-e-furqat agar bura na lage (4)
bahut hi saada hai tu aur zamana hai ayaar
khuda kare ki tujhe shahr ki hava na lage
bujha na den ye musalsal udaasiyan dil ko
vo baat kar ki tabiyat ko taaziyana lage

वो इस अदा से जो आये तो क्यों भला न लगे
हज़ार बार मिलो फिर भी दूसरा न लगे
कभी वो ख़ास इनायत कि सौ गुमाँ गुज़रें
कभी वो तर्ज़-ए-तग़ाफ़ुल कि मुजरिमाना लगे
वो सीधी सादी अदाएँ कि बिजलियाँ बरसें
वो दिलबराना मुरव्वत कि आशिक़ाना लगे
दिखाऊँ दाग़-ए-मुहब्बत जो नागवार न हो
सुनाऊँ क़िस्सा-ए-फ़ुरकत अगर बुरा न लगे (4)
बहुत ही सादा है तू और ज़माना है अय्यार
ख़ुदा करे कि तुझे शहर की हवा न लगे
बुझा न दें ये मुसलसल उदासियाँ दिल को
वो बात कर कि तबीयत को ताज़ियाना लगे

--*continue*—

91. Why wouldn't it feel good the way she came

Why wouldn't it feel good the way she came
Meet her a thousand times, it's all the same

With kindness, she can give a myriad illusion
With her disinterest a feeling of persecution

Her naive, artless ways strike like lightning
Her intimate concerns make signs of loving

I can show scars of love, if it is not unkind
Tell tales of our parting if you don't mind (4)

You are innocent and the world full of guile
God spare you from the city's wind and vile

Lest this relentless misery make me clam up
Say something that will sting me like a whip
                              --continue--

91. vo is ada se jo aaye to kyun bhala na lage

jo ghar ujad gaye un ka na ranj kar pyare
vo chara kar ki ye gulshan ujaad sa na lage
itaab-e-ahl-e-jahan sab bhula diye lekin
vo zakhm yaad hain ab tak jo ghayabana lage (8)
vo rang dil ko diye hain lahu ki gardish ne
nazar uthaun to duniya nigaarkhana lage
ajeeb khwab dikhaate hain nakhuda ham ko
gharaz ye hai ki safina kinare ja na lage
liye hi jaati hai hardam koyi sada 'nasir'
ye aur baat suragh-e-nishan-e-paa na lage

जो घर उजड़ गये उनका न रंज कर प्यारे
वो चारा कर कि ये गुलशन उजाड़-सा न लगे
इताब-ए-अह्ल-ए-जहाँ सब भुला दिये लेकिन
वो ज़ख़्म याद हैं अब तक जो ग़ायबाना लगे (8)
वो रंग दिल को दिये हैं लहू की गर्दिश ने
नज़र उठाऊँ तो दुनिया निग़ारख़ाना लगे
अजीब ख़्वाब दिखाते हैं नाख़ुदा हमको
ग़रज़ ये है कि सफ़ीना किनारे जा न लगे
लिए ही जाती है हर दम कोई सदा 'नासिर'
ये और बात सुराग़-ए-निशाने-पा न लगे

91. Why wouldn't it feel good the way she came

Don't bother for nests that were wrecked
Make sure this garden does not get ravaged

I have all forgotten the worldly blows to me
But not the deep hits that lie buried in me (8)

Blood in veins endowed the heart such hues
That eyes see this world a gallery of statues

My boatman charms me with a dreamy lore
To make sure the boat lands not at the shore.

A call keeps me going 'Nasir' all the times
Though it has no footprints or visible signs

92. *vo sahilon pe gaane vaale kya huye*

vo sahilon pe gaane vaale kya huye
vo kashtiyan chalaane vaale kya huye
vo subah aate aate rah gayi kahan
jo qafile the aane vaale kya huye
main un ki raah dekhta hun raat bhar
vo roshni dikhaane vaale kya huye
ye kaun log hain mere idhar udhar
vo dosti nibhaane vaale kya huye (4)
vo dil men khubne vaali aankhen kya huyin
vo honth muskuraane vaale kya huye
imaaraten to jal ke raakh ho gayin
imaaraten banaane vaale kya huye
akele ghar se puchhti hai bekasi
tera diya jalaane vaale kya huye
ye aap ham to bojh hain zameen ka
zamin ka bojh uthaane vaale kya huye (8)

वो साहिलों पे गाने वाले क्या हुए
वो कश्तियाँ चलाने वाले क्या हुए
वो सुब्ह आते-आते रह गयी कहाँ
जो क़ाफ़िले थे आने वाले क्या हुए
मैं उनकी राह देखता हूँ रात-भर
वो रोशनी दिखाने वाले क्या हुए
ये कौन लोग हैं मिरे इधर-उधर
वो दोस्ती निभाने वाले क्या हुए (4)
वो दिल में खुबने वाली आँखें क्या हुईं
वो होंठ मुस्कराने वाले क्या हुए
इमारतें तो जलके राख़ हो गईं
इमारतें बनाने वाले क्या हुए
अकेले घर से पूछती है बेकसी
तिरा दिया जलाने वाले क्या हुए
ये आप हम तो बोझ हैं ज़मीन का
ज़मीं का बोझ उठाने वाले क्या हुए (8)

92. Those who sang on the banks, where are they

Those who sang on the banks, where are they
Those who rowed the boats, where are they

Where is the morning we've been waiting for
The caravans we expected, where are they

The whole night I look up their way, who
Were once our torchbearer, where are they

Who are these people that surround me
The folks that knew loyalty, where are they (4)

The eyes that shot through my heart
The lips that flashed smiles, where are they

The buildings turned to ash after the flames
The hands that build them, where are they

Misery that dwells in the lonely house asks
Those who kept it lighted, where are they

You and I are sheer burden on this earth
Those who carry the earth, where are they (8)

93. *yaad aata hai roz-o-shab koyi*

yaad aata hai roz-o-shab koyi
ham se rootha hai besabab koyi
lab-e-ju chhanv men darakhton ki
vo mulaqaat thi ajab koyi
jab tujhe pahli baar dekha tha
vo bhi tha mausam-e-tarab koyi
kuchh khabar le ki teri mahfil se
door baitha hai jaan-ba-lab koyi (4)
na gham-e-zindagi na dard-e-firaq
dil men yun hi si hai talab koyi
yaad aati hain dur ki baaten
pyaar se dekhta hai jab koyi
chot khaayi hai barha lekin
aaj to dard hai ajab koyi
jin ko mitna tha mit chuke 'nasir'
un ko rusva kare na ab koyi (8)

याद आता है रोज़-ओ-शब कोई
हमसे रूठा है बेसबब कोई
लब-ए-जू छाँव में दरख़्तों की
वो मुलाक़ात थी अजब कोई
जब तुझे पहली बार देखा था
वो भी था मौसम-ए-तरब कोई
कुछ ख़बर ले कि तेरी महफ़िल से
दूर बैठा है जाँ-ब-लब कोई (4)
न ग़म-ए-ज़िंदगी न दर्द-ए-फ़िराक
दिल में यूँ ही सी है तलब कोई
याद आती हैं दूर की बातें
प्यार से देखता है जब कोई
चोट खाई है बारहा लेकिन
आज तो दर्द है अजब कोई
जिनको मिटना था मिट चुके 'नासिर'
उनको रुसवा करे न अब कोई (8)

93. I long to see someone night and day

I long to see someone night and day
Who for no reason just turned away

Riverside under the shade of a tree
What an amazing meeting used to be

When I saw you for the first time
What joy it was and a pleasant clime

Do attend to the one sitting far away
With baited breath waiting your way (4)

No worldly worries, no pangs of parting
Yet the heart aches with a dark longing

I get nostalgic about days long gone by
When someone casts a loving eye

Many times earlier, I have been hurt
But pain today is something unheard

'Nasir' those destined to die, have left
Let no one now hold them in contempt (8)

94. *ye bhi kya shaam-e-mulaqaat aayi*

ye bhi kya shaam-e-mulaqaat aayi
lab pe mushkil se teri baat aayi
subah se chup hain tere hijr-naseeb
haaye kya hoga agar raat aayi
bastiyan chhod ke barse badal
kis qayamat ki ye barsaat aayi
koyi jab mil ke huya tha rukhsat
dil-e-betab vahi raat aayi (4)
saya-e-zulf-e-butan men 'nasir'
ek se ek nayi raat aayi

ये भी क्या शाम-ए-मुलाक़ात आयी
लब पे मुश्किल से तिरी बात आयी
सुब्ह से चुप हैं तिरे हिज्र-नसीब
हाय क्या होगा अगर रात आयी
बस्तियाँ छोड़ के बरसे बादल
किस क़यामत की ये बरसात आयी
कोई जब मिल के हुआ था रुख़सत
दिल-ए-बेताब वही रात आयी
साया-ए-ज़ुल्फ़-ए-बुताँ में 'नासिर'
एक से एक नयी रात आयी

94. What an evening it was to meet

What an evening it was to meet
When I barely had anything to speak

Dejected, I lie in silence since morning
What happens, if the night is a repeat?

Clouds poured rains away from cities
What disaster this rain would wreak

When someone met and departed
O my heart! Tonight is the same beat (4)

Under the beauty's dark tresses 'Nasir'
Every night was a new night to greet.

95. ye raat tumhari hai chamakte raho taaro

ye raat tumhari hai chamakte raho taaro
vo aayen na aayen magar umeed na haaro
shayad kisi manzil se koyi qafila aaye
ashufta-saro subah talak yun hi pukaaro
din bhar to chale ab zara dam le ke chalenge
ai hamsafaro aaj yahin raat guzaaro
ye alam-e-vahshat hai to kuchh ho hi rahega
manzil na sahi sar kisi deewar se maaro (4)
ojhal huye jaate hain nigaahon se do aalam
tum aaj kahan ho gham-e-furqat ke sahaaro
khoya hai use jis ka badal koyi nahin hai
ye baat magar kaun sune laakh pukaaro

ये रात तुम्हारी है चमकते रहो तारो
वो आएँ न आएँ मगर उम्मीद न हारो
शायद किसी मंज़िल से कोई क़ाफ़िला आए
आशुफ़्ता-सरो सुब्ह तलक यूँही पुकारो
दिन भर तो चले अब ज़रा दम ले के चलेंगे
ऐ हम-सफ़रो आज यहीं रात गुज़ारो
ये आलम-ए-वहशत है तो कुछ हो ही रहेगा
मंज़िल न सही सर किसी दीवार से मारो (4)
ओझल हुए जाते हैं निगाहों से दो आलम
तुम आज कहाँ हो ग़म-ए-फ़ुर्क़त के सहारो
खोया है उसे जिस का बदल कोई नहीं है
ये बात मगर कौन सुने लाख पुकारो

95. O stars! The night is all yours, keep shining

O stars! The night is all yours, keep shining
Whether he shows up or not, keep shining

You may find somewhere a caravan coming
O you road-weary! Keep calling till morning

Walking the whole day, let's halt for a respite
Fellow travellers! Here today spend the night

In this mood of madness, anything may befall
If not the destination, hit head against a wall (4)

My vision of both the worlds is getting fuzzy
Where are those who stood by me in misery

We have lost something that has no equal
But who cares even if thousand times I tell

96. *ye shab ye khayal-o-khwab tere*

ye shab ye khayal-o-khwab tere
kya phool khile hain munh andhere
sholay men hai ek rang tera
baaqi hain tamaam rang mere
ankhon men chhupaaye phir raha hun
yadon ke bujhe huye savere
dete hain suraagh fasl-e-gul ka
shakhon pe jale hue basere (4)
manzil na mili to qafilon ne
raste men jamaa liye hain dere
jangal men huyi hai shaam ham ko
basti se chale the munh-andhere
rudaad-e-safar na chhed 'nasir'
phir ashk na tham sakenge mere

ये शब ये ख़याल-ओ-ख़्वाब तेरे
क्या फूल खिले हैं मुँह-अँधेरे
शोले में है एक रंग तेरा
बाक़ी हैं तमाम रंग मेरे
आँखों में छुपाए फिर रहा हूँ
यादों के बुझे हुए सवेरे
देते हैं सुराग़ फ़स्ल-ए-गुल का
शाख़ों पे जले हुए बसेरे (4)
मंज़िल न मिली तो क़ाफ़िलों ने
रस्ते में जमा लिए हैं डेरे
जंगल में हुई है शाम हम को
बस्ती से चले थे मुँह-अँधेरे
रूदाद-ए-सफ़र न छेड़ 'नासिर'
फिर अश्क न थम सकेंगे मेरे

96. Images, dreams of you at night

Images, dreams of you at night
Are like flowers in morning light

Flame has one colour of yours
Rest of all are mine, of course

In my eyes forever are hidden
Mornings of the days forgotten

The charred twigs and nests tell
The harvest of flowers that fell (4)

When caravans march saw no end
They settled around the bend

We started from town early morn
Landed by eve in a jungle forlorn

'Nasir' don't start on journey's woes
Tears that follow I can't stop those

97. ye sitam aur ki ham phool kahen kharon ko

ye sitam aur ki ham phool kahen khaaron ko
is se to aag hi lag jaaye samanzaaron ko
hai abas fikr-e-talafi tujhe ai jaan-e-wafa
dhun hai ab aur hi kuchh tere talabgaaron ko
tanha tanha hi guzari hain andheri raaten
ham ne ghabra ke pukaara na kabhi taaron ko
nagahaan phoot pade roshniyon ke jharne
ek jhonka hi uda le gaya andhiyaaron ko (4)
saare is daur ki munh bolti tasveeren hain
koyi dekhe mere deewan ke kirdaaron ko
nala-e-aakhir-e-shab kis ko sunaun 'nasir'
neend pyaari hai mere daur ke fankaaron ko

ये सितम और कि हम फूल कहें ख़ारों को
इस से तो आग ही लग जाए समन-ज़ारों को
है अबस फ़िक्र-ए-तलाफ़ी तुझे ऐ जान-ए-वफ़ा
धुन है अब और ही कुछ तेरे तलब-गारों को
तन-ए-तन्हा ही गुज़ारी हैं अँधेरी रातें
हम ने घबरा के पुकारा न कभी तारों को
ना-गहाँ फूट पड़े रौशनियों के झरने
एक झोंका ही उड़ा ले गया अँधियारों को (4)
सारे इस दौर की मुँह बोलती तस्वीरें हैं
कोई देखे मिरे दीवान के किरदारों को
नाला-ए-आख़िर-ए-शब किस को सुनाऊँ 'नासिर'
नींद प्यारी है मिरे दौर के फ़नकारों को

97. Cruel it is, if we are asked to call spikes flowers

Cruel it is, if we are asked to call spikes flowers
I would rather have fire on such fields of flowers

We regret, dear loyalty, for going against you
Your lovers are now bent on some new honours

I have spent dark nights many a time by myself
Never have I asked in despair stars for covers

All of a sudden, beams of light come cascading
With one big sweep the mist of darkness clears (4)

All of them are well known portraits of our times
If you take a look at my anthology of characters

Who should 'Nasir' sing for last dirge of the night
For sleep in our times is dear to our songsters

98. *yun tere husn ki tasveer ghazal men aaye*

yun tere husn ki tasveer ghazal men aaye
jaise bilqis suleman ke mahal men aaye
jabr se ek hua zayeqa-e-hijr-o-visal
ab kahan se vo maza sabr ke phal men aaye
ye bhi araaish-e-hasti ka taqaaza tha ki ham
halqa-e-fikr se maidan-e-amal men aaye
har qadam dast-o-gareban hai yahan khair se shar
ham bhi kis maarka-e-jang-o-jadal men aaye (4)
zindagi jin ke tasavvur se jila paati thi
haaye kya log the jo daam-e-ajal men aaye

यूँ तिरे हुस्न की तस्वीर ग़ज़ल में आए
जैसे बिल्क़ीस सुलेमाँ के महल में आए
जब्र से एक हुआ ज़ाएक़ा-ए-हिज्र-ओ-विसाल
अब कहाँ से वो मज़ा सब्र के फल में आए
ये भी आराइश-ए-हस्ती का तक़ाज़ा था कि हम
हल्क़ा-ए-फ़िक्र से मैदान-ए-अमल में आए
हर क़दम दस्त-ओ-गरेबाँ है यहाँ ख़ैर से शर
हम भी किस मारका-ए-जंग-ओ-जदल में आए (4)
ज़िंदगी जिन के तसव्वुर से जिला पाती थी
हाए क्या लोग थे जो दाम-ए-अजल में आए

98. Portrait of your beauty enters into my verse

Portrait of your beauty enters into my verse
The way queen Bilkis enters Suleman's palace

Meeting and parting have same pleasure in haste
Where now is the fruit of patience and its taste?

This too was the demand of the celebration of life
That we moved from the abstract to practical life

Every step is a fist fight between good and evil
What is it that we have come to - a field of battle? (4)

Reminiscing about them alone brings to life shine
What amazing people who fell to the trap of time

99. *zaban sukhan ko sukhan bankpan ko tarsega*

zaban sukhan ko sukhan bankpan ko tarsega
sukhankada meri tarz-e-sukhan ko tarsega
naye piyaale sahi tere daur men saaqi
ye daur meri sharab-e-kuhan ko tarsega
mujhe to khair vatan chhod kar amaan na mili
vatan bhi mujh se gharibul-vatan ko tarsega
inhi ke dam se farozan hain millaton ke charagh
zamana sohbat-e-arbaab-e-fan ko tarsega (4)
badal sako to badal do ye baghbaan varna
ye baagh saya-e-sarv-o-saman ko tarsega
hava-e-zulm yahi hai to dekhna ik din
zamin paani ko suraj kiran ko tarsega

ज़बाँ सुख़न को, सुख़न बाँकपन को तरसेगा
सुख़नकदा मिरी तर्ज़-ए-सुख़न को तरसेगा
नये पियाले सही, तेरे दौर में साक़ी
ये दौर मेरी शराब-ए-कुहन को तरसेगा
मुझे तो ख़ैर वतन छोड़कर अमाँ न मिली
वतन भी मुझसे ग़ारीबुल-वतन को तरसेगा
उन्हीं के दम से फ़रोज़ाँ हैं मिल्लतों के चिराग़
ज़माना सोहबत-ए-अरबाब-ए-फ़न को तरसेगा (4)
बदल सको तो बदल दो ये बाग़बाँ वरना
ये बाग़ साया-ए-सर्व-ओ-समन को तरसेगा
हवा-ए-ज़ुल्म यही है तो देखना इक दिन
ज़मीन पानी को, सूरज किरन को तरसेगा

99. Speech will long for words and words for delicacy

Speech will long for words and words for delicacy
The house of verse will long for my kind of poetry

Your bar may have new wineglasses in these times
But this age too will cherish my type of old whiskey

Though I found little peace on leaving my country
My homeland too will look for an émigré like me

Communities stay enlightened because of them
The world shall miss artists and their company (4)

You must change the gardener, if you can, else
The garden will miss shade of flowers and a tree

If the wave of tyranny persists, the Earth for water,
The Sun for its rays will cry one day, you will see

100. Assorted verses from *Pehli Baarish*

din kaa phool abhi jaaga tha
dhoop kaa haath baḍha aata tha
teri khamoshi ki shah paakar
main kitni baaten karta tha
teri hilal si ungli pakde
main koson paidal chalta tha
ankhon men teri shakl chhupaye
main sab se chhupta phirta tha (4)
raat gaye sone se pahle
tune mujha se kuchh poochha tha
Yun guzari vo raat bhee jaise
sapane men sapana dekha tha
Aankh khuli to tujhe na paakar
main kitana bechain huya tha
 tere angan ke pichhvade
sabz darakhton ka ramna tha (8)
 bhooli nahin us raat ki dahshat
charkh pe jab taara tuta tha

दिन का फूल अभी जागा था
धूप का हाथ बढ़ा आता था
तेरी ख़ामोशी की शह पाकर
मैं कितनी बातें करता था
तेरी हिलाल-सी उँगली पकड़े
मैं कोसों पैदल चलता था
आँखों में तिरी शक्ल छुपाये
मैं सबसे छुपता फिरता था (4)
रात गये सोने से पहले
तूने मुझसे कुछ पूछा था
यूँ गुज़री वो रात भी जैसे
सपने में सपना देखा था
आँख खुली तो तुझे न पाकर
मैं कितना बेचैन हुआ था
तेरे आँगन के पिछवाड़े
सब्ज़ दरख़्तों का रमना था (8)
भूली नहीं उस रात की दहशत
चर्ख़ पे जब तारा टूटा था

100. Assorted verses from *Pehli Baarish*

The day like a flower just showed
The sun was making moves bold

Under the cover of your silence
How many things about me I told

Holding your moon-like finger
Miles and many miles I strode

Hiding your figure in my eyes
I hid myself from the world (4)

 Before going to sleep last night
Something in my ears you told

That night too I spent as if
Dream within a dream I behold

Not finding you, when I woke up
I found myself left in the cold

At the back of your courtyard
Trees made a cool green holt (8)

I can't ever get over that terror
When in the sky a star rolled

www.ingramcontent.com/pod-product-compliance
Lightning Source LLC
LaVergne TN
LVHW061608070526
838199LV00078B/7211